DATE DUE

JUL 1 6 2005	
AUG 1 4 2006	
NOV 3 0 2007	
AUG 1 9 2008	
SEP 1 4 2010	
JUN 0 1 2015	
JUL 1 6 2015	
DEC 0 3 2015	

GAYLORD

PRINTED IN U.S.A.

Fermentation
and Winemaking Methods

Pierre Drapeau and André Vanasse

THE ENCYCLOPEDIA OF HOME WINEMAKING

I. Fermentation and Winemaking Methods

Translated by
Darcy Dunton

XYZ
Publishing

5/02

Second printing, 2001.

© XYZ Publishing
1781 St. Hubert Street
Montreal, (Quebec)
H2L 3Z1
Telephone: (514) 525-9518
Fax: (514) 525-7537
E-mail: xyzed@mlink.net

and

Pierre Drapeau

and

André Vanasse

Legal deposit: 2nd quarter, 1998
National Library of Canada
Bibliothèque nationale du Québec
ISBN 0-9683601-0-6

Distributed in Canada and in the United States by:
General Distribution Services (GDS)
325 Humber College Boulevard
Toronto, Ontario   M9W 7C3
Tel: (416) 213-1919
Fax: (416) 213-1917
E-Mail : cservice@genpub.com

Typesetting concept and layout: Édiscript enr.
Cover design: Zirval Design
Cover photograph: Ludovic Fremaux

Table of Contents

Chapter 4
The Basic Equipment and How to Use It

Chapter 7
Measurements, Scales and Tests

Chapter 8
Grape Varieties and Home-Made Wine

The publication of this book was made possible by a grant from Mosti Mondiale Inc., importers, producers, and wholesalers of musts for home winemaking.

Mosti Mondiale Inc.

6865 Route 132
St. Catherine (Quebec), Canada
J0L 1E0
Telephone: (450) 638-6380
Fax: (450) 638-7049
Internet Site Address: www.mostimondiale.com

Acknowledgments

Pierre Drapeau and André Vanasse would like to thank Darcy Dunton for her excellent translation.

They also express their deep appreciation to the staff at Mosti Mondiale, especially:

- Marc Moran, without whom this project could not have been undertaken. His enthusiasm and generous help and advice allowed this book to be completed in the best possible circumstances;
- Nino Piazza, who kindly and spontaneously offered Mosti Mondiale's technical assistance as well as its testing laboratories;
- Sigrid Gertsen-Briand, for her generous technological assistance.

Pierre Drapeau would like to pay a particular tribute to:
- his two most important collaborators, his wife Rita and his son Pascal, who both devoted themselves unstintingly to allow him to finish this book;
- his customers, who have continually inspired him to carry out further research and to obtain the most up-to-date information to answer a thousand questions concerning the art of winemaking;
- his students, always eager to learn more and to hone their knowledge;
- all the store-owners who have dedicated part of their lives to the defense and the dissemination of the great and noble activity that is winemaking.

André Vanasse wishes to thank:
- Dr. Michel Vanasse, who parted (temporarily!) with his library collection on oenology, a vast and complex area of human knowledge.

The authors would like to thank the following distribution companies for having provided the material for the photographs free of charge: ABC CORK, Distrivin, Divin Distribution, Microvin, Mosti Mondiale, Spagnol's, Vineco International Products, Vinothèque, and Wine-Art. We also thank the Microvin store, Lallemand Laboratories, and Lalvin yeast makers for providing material to illustrate this book.

CHAPTER ONE

Grapes and Wine

A t an unknown point lost in the mists of time, human beings began to make wine from grapes. Wine is mentioned in innumerable ancient writings, including hundreds of biblical passages. The habit of drinking wine was undoubtedly acquired by the Hebrews before Moses led them from Egypt. The Egyptians, in turn, had likely been initiated to it by the Persians while the latter occupied Mesopotamia. The Persians themselves would have learned it from the Sumerians, allowing us to attribute a respectable antiquity of at least six thousand years to winemaking. The museum at the Mouton-Rothschild estate contains proof of this, with its winemaking artifacts dating from the third millenium B.C.

As to who actually discovered the secret of making wine, we can only assume that its heady delights were accidentally discovered when someone negligently left some grape juice standing too long.

However, to make wine properly, the fermentation process had to be scientifically understood. This knowledge must have developed through trial and error until the winemaking process was mastered sufficiently to produce a justifiable quantity of good wine every year.

This was achieved by techniques which are still practised today. For example, the use of sulphur (contained in sulphur dioxide) for protecting wine from contaminants and oxidation was already known to the Greeks. It is difficult to say if this practice had been handed down by more ancient civilizations. We do know, however, that sulphur was used to disinfect clothes in ancient China.

Amphorae over a thousand years old have been recovered from the Mediterranean Sea, containing what can still be recognized as wine, proving that the ancients not only knew how to make wine, but also how to preserve it.

Greek amphora at the Museo Nazionale di Napoli, showing cherubs harvesting and crushing grapes.

Grapes: Their Composition and Properties

Does wine possess superior virtues over alcoholic beverages made from other fruits? Judging by its fame and fortune in the temperate regions of half the world, it would appear so. The reason for this is certainly related to the nature of the grape whose constituent elements are in harmonious balance, making the resulting beverage infinitely more pleasant to drink than those based on other fruit, cider for example, which has a much more acidic taste.

The following illustration gives a breakdown of the grape's different properties. The fruit, attached to the stalk (or stem), is made up of:

a) a thin outer layer, the skin;

b) an inner part (by far the most important) called the pulp, that is, the "flesh" of the grape;

c) the seeds, which vary in proportion according to the variety and size of the grape.

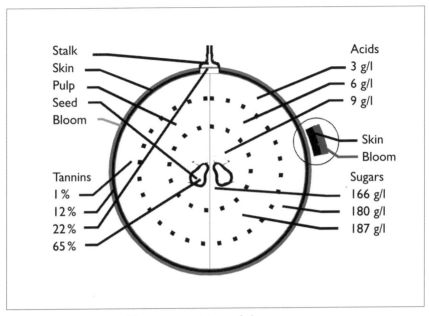

The composition of the grape.

All of these constituent elements are of enormous importance in winemaking, precisely because wine is composed first and foremost of acids, sugar, and tannin, besides the distinct flavour characteristics given to it by the fruit.

The Pulp of the Grape

As we have pointed out, the pulp is the essential part of the grape, making up 95 % of the fruit. The pulp contains the acids, sugars, and numerous mineral salts and other organic components which give the grape its particular taste and aroma. For every variety of grape possesses subtle differences in flavour, and certain varieties make better wines than others. This is so true that a must [1] of Chardonnay grapes costs much more than a must of Thompson Seedless, to give just one

---

1. The term "must" designates grape juice destined to become wine.

example. In many cases, it is both a question of flavour and of yield: often, the most sought-after grapes grow less profusely on the vine, but have a richer concentration of juice. In some countries, laws exist limiting the amount of grapes per vine and per hectare that wine-growers are permitted to culti-vate if they wish to retain their title to an *appellation*.

Along with these basic factors, the quality of wine depends to a large extent on the amount of rainfall that the grapes receive as they ripen: the more rain, the greater the chance that the grapes will become engorged with water, with a resulting loss of flavour intensity. Inversely, long dry periods produce just as seri-ous an imbalance among the

The grape is the raw material of wine.

components as too much rain does. The desirable proportions for wine grapes are considered to be 75 % water and 20 % sugar (with the remaining 5 % consisting of all the other organic components, in particular, the acids which play such an important role in the transformation of the grape). Thus, there are good and bad years for making wine.

The climatic influence is, moreover, so crucial in wine production that the producers of *grands crus* usually make less wine in a bad year. They do this to protect their reputations as fine wine-growers, using only the best grapes in the elabora-tion of the *grandes appellations*. The rest of the grapes har-vested have their rating lowered and are used for the lesser *appellations*.

The Seeds and the Tannin

Grape seeds contain a large amount of tannin, a bitter-tasting substance which spreads through the wine as it ferments. The tannin is what gives wine its astringency (creating a dry, puckery sensation on the palate, the gums, the tongue, and the other tissues of the mouth). However, it also contributes much to the wine's flavour, to its preservation, and to its clarification after fermentation. The wines that age best always have a high tannin content. Red wines contain ten times as much tannin as white wines: we will explain how this occurs further on.

The Grapeskin

The grapeskin's role in winemaking is far from negligible. The skin is very often covered by a fine velvety powder called the bloom, which contains bacteria that affect the taste of the finished wine. The bloom also usually holds some yeasts which participate in the fermentation process. It is, moreover, due to the action of these yeasts that wine fermented in the past. The use of yeasts selected in laboratories to activate and to guarantee the fermentation of wine is a recent development: before that, only the natural yeasts from the bloom could induce fermentation. Today, cultured yeasts are increasingly used to invigorate fermentation and to make it more predictable. Specific yeasts have been identified as the best for a high-quality fermentation. In fact, these yeasts are now cultivated in bulk in the laboratory.

Surprisingly, the pulp of both red and so-called white grapes is the same colour, that is, a very pale, translucent green. There are a few notable exceptions: some grapes have a red pulp. These are called tinting grapes (*raisins teinturiers*) and produce only red wines, whereas all other red grape varieties can be used to make either red or white wine. They will only produce red wines if their skins are kept in the fermenting must to provide the necessary pigment to colour the wine.

This was one of the problems that had to be solved before people began marketing fresh musts for home winemaking. The musts sold commercially contain only the juice, without any grape residue whatsoever; therefore they have to be pigmented beforehand. Normally, pigmentation occurs during the first

Yeast is essential for fermentation. Today, laboratory-cultured yeasts are used.

few days of fermentation. To prevent the must from fermenting during the pigmentation process (which would make its sale illegal under present laws), one of the solutions in the past was to heat it, as is done for sterilized concentrated must. This technique is resorted to less and less frequently. To keep all of the must's flavour intact, a better method is to add metabisulphite while simultaneously lowering the temperature. Colour-boosting (adding the juice of tinting grapes) may be carried out if necessary.

A bunch of *Vitis vinifera*, drawn by the great botanist, Linnaeus.

For a few years now, the Mosti Mondiale company, in the business of importing, producing and selling must for home winemaking, has been offering amateur winemakers the opportunity to pigment their own musts. The company imports special-edition musts from Sonoma (California), in season, together with the grapeskins. The amateur winemaker should then proceed as in the method for making wine from whole grapes, that is, the "cap" formed by the grape residue has to be "punched down" into the wine at least twice a day to impart pigment and tannin to the must. This new method, halfway between the traditional process, which starts with pressing the grapes, and making wine with must purchased from the retailer, has gained considerable favour among the most experienced home vintners.

Grape Varieties

Innumerable species of grapes exist, as the grapevine has adapted to almost all of the world's inhabitable climates. When the first explorers arrived in Canada, they were surprised to discover native grapevines (hence the Vinland of the Vikings), which were not, unfortunately, appropriate for making wine (the attempt was made, but their fruit produced a very bitter wine). Of the approximately 5000 species of grapes that have been classified (the grapevine has been around for more than 40 million years!), only about 250 are suitable for making wine.

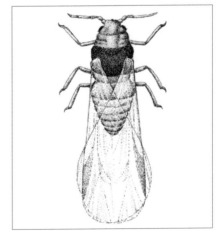

Phylloxera, the vintner's worst enemy.

The unsuitability of New World grapevines for vinification purposes was precisely the reason that some of the noble European varieties were grafted onto them to improve the quality and the taste of the wine made from their fruit. In 1864, during grafting experiments carried out in the Gard region of southern France, an aphid known as phylloxera was unwittingly brought over on American vines, and quickly revealed itself as the worst enemy of vintners since the origins of winemaking. This aphid, which feeds on the grapevine's sap, especially that of the roots, spread like the bubonic plague, destroying almost all the vineyards of France, before moving on to the rest of Europe, North Africa, and even Australia and New Zealand. The damage that it caused to wine production was unprecedented. Thousands of wineries were ruined: in France alone, losses to vineyard owners were estimated at almost two billion gold francs, an absolutely colossal sum! This episode is a striking illustration of what can happen without the regulations that we have today, which control how plants and other agricultural products are brought from one country to another.

After dozens of desperate and fruitless attempts to eradicate the phylloxera, there appeared to be only one solution: the importation of phylloxera-resistant American grapevines (the wines made from these were abhorred by most Europeans), so that French vines could be grafted on to them, in hopes that the resulting fruit would conserve the characteristics of the original French grapes. Happily, it worked, but the entire thousand-year-old French wine industry had to be rebuilt from scratch.

Grape Varieties and Climatic Variation

French wine grapes are the most famous: almost everyone is familiar with the names of noble varieties like Chardonnay, Merlot, Cabernet Sauvignon, Cabernet Franc, Sauvignon Blanc, Pinot Noir, Chenin Blanc, and Gamay. There are also dozens of other French grape varieties that produce exceptional wines: Riesling, Gewürztraminer, Mourvèdre, Syrah, Sylvaner, and Tocai. There remain some highly respectable varieties like Asti, Carignan, Cinsaut, Barbera, Muscat, Nebbiolo,

Sangiovese and Chasselas. For more details on the varieties used most often in the musts and concentrates available to home winemakers, a descriptive list makes up most of Chapter 8 of this book.

Depending on where it is planted, a grape variety will absorb its specific character from the soil and the climate. To

Chardonnay grapes, an extremely popular variety these days.

give an example, the taste of Chardonnay wine differs according to whether the vines are grown in France, the United States, or Australia. In general, wine produced from the same grape variety will have more body if grown in a warmer climate, and be more mellow if grown in a cooler one. Also speaking generally, the best wines are produced in a temperate climate, which explains why warm regions like southern Italy, Greece, or North Africa are not known for producing fine wines, whereas France and Germany are considered the countries in which the best wine in the world is made.

Over the last few decades, winemakers have proved that excellent wines can be produced in California. California wines have even won out over their French counterparts in blind tasting sessions (in which the tasters do not know the names or origins of the wines).

California wine grapes, however, are not of equal quality throughout the state. The Department of Viticulture at the Davis campus of the University of California, an institute specializing in wine research, has divided California into different climatic regions based on the average number of warm days during the year. Thus, Regions I, II, and III, cooled as they are by sea winds, have climates comparable to certain wine-producing regions of France, Germany, and northern Italy, while Regions IV and V have summers like those of Naples or Algiers. It goes without saying that the wines produced in Regions I to III, for example, those of the Sonoma and Napa Valleys, are clearly superior to wines produced around San Joaquin, in the hot Region V, where huge quantities of grapes are grown.

Obviously, the quality of the musts imported from California depends to a large degree on the region where the grapes are grown. Then, even if the grapes come from the more reputed regions, there is nothing to guarantee that they were among the best grapes picked! Let's be honest: it might be a long time before you can compete with the great Mondavi wines (some of which cost a modest $100 a bottle!).

The fact is, importers of musts can choose among different regions and among different qualities of wine grapes, but they seldom have access to the grapes of the most reputed vineyards. In any case, even if they could obtain them, the price of the musts would be prohibitive.

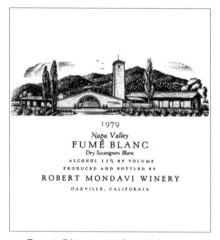

Fumé Blanc, produced by the Robert Mondavi Winery, one of California's best wine-growers. (Napa Valley, Region II)

The majority of the imported fresh musts and wine grapes available to home winemakers are from California, but there is also a choice of products from Italy, Australia, Chile, Argentina, Spain, France, South Africa, and Germany.

CHAPTER 2

Fermentation

fter the grapes are picked, they must be fermented. This is a delicate operation which must be carried out carefully, observing very strict standards, or the wine will oxidate and go bad. The rule of paramount importance which cannot be stressed enough is hygiene, because wine in the process of fermenting is very sensitive to bacteria.

The phenomenon of fermentation has been scientifically understood for at least a century and a half, thanks to research done by Louis Pasteur. He was the first to conclude that the fermentation of wine was a result of the action of yeasts. With Pasteur's fantastic discovery, it was finally possible to comprehend and to master the chemical process that occurs during the fermentation of wine.

Yeasts

Essential in making wine, yeasts are living one-cell organisms which reproduce spontaneously. The most appropriate yeasts for winemaking belong to the *Saccharomyces* family, which includes the yeasts used for baking bread and brewing beer.

If it is true that yeasts are found naturally on the surface of the grape, it is not true that they arise spontaneously: these micro-organisms are borne through the air and settle on the grapes. They are also carried onto the grapes by the insects that come to gather nectar from the vines.

Yeasts cannot be created synthetically. It is possible, however, to cultivate them in the laboratory, and to stimulate their reproduction, resulting in large quantities of yeast.

More than 2000 species of yeast are known. They are classified by their form (round or oval) and by their specific properties. Yeasts that are appropriate for winemaking are oval, round, or elliptical.

Wine yeasts feed on sugar (saccharose). When it is absorbed by the yeast, sugar is transformed into alcohol and carbon dioxide. Depending on the type of yeast, this process also gives forth chemical by-products (considered waste) which are not always desirable in the transformation of the must into wine. Some yeasts give the wine a bad taste. This is why it is necessary to use only wine yeasts and to avoid others, particularly bread yeast.

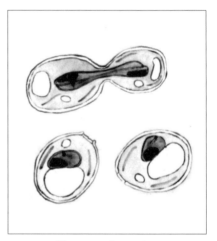

Yeasts cells under the microscope.

Moreover, the acetobacters deposited by fruit flies can cause an acerbic astringency which makes the wine taste like vinegar. Metabisulphite kills the bacteria and allows the appropriate yeasts to restart fermentation; the next chapter will give more details on this.

Scientific progress has allowed the development of selected yeasts in the laboratory according to the type of wine to be produced. However, we shouldn't delude ourselves: the properties of yeasts are completely unrelated to particular grape varieties. They only serve in pursuing the specific goals that the winemaker has in mind. Certain yeasts produce higher degrees of alcohol than others (many yeasts die or become inactive when the alcoholic content reaches 14 percent or 28 degrees Proof). Other yeasts possess other distinctive properties which can be exploited to advantage by knowledgeable amateur vintners.

To give an example: if you intend to make a wine for drinking young, a 71B-1122 yeast (Saccharomyces cerevisiae) *is recommended, because it will rapidly bring out the intrinsic qualities of your wine. On the other hand, if you want to make a sparkling wine, it is advised to use EC-1118* (Saccharomyces bayanus): *this yeast tolerates a high degree of alcohol and is therefore more suitable for making sparkling wines. Finally, the K1-V1116 type of yeast is used very often for red wines: it has the ability to absorb all the oxygen in the wine during its reproductive phase, thus asphyxiating the wild yeasts that might be present.*

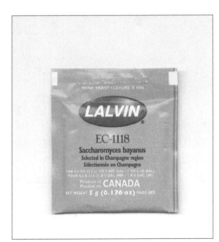

The EC-1118 type is a resistant yeast and one of the most popular.

About forty types of wine yeasts are now produced, sufficient for the needs of both the industry and the amateur winemaker. The world leader in this domain is Lallemand & Co., with its head office in Montreal.

During laboratory experiments, it was also discovered that certain yeasts adapt better to variations in the alcohol content of wine as they pass from one generation to another. The first generation may live quite comfortably with a specific gravity of 1.070 [1]

---

1. On density measurement, see the description of the hydrometer in Chapter 4.

while the following generation is more comfortable with a specific gravity of 1.050 and a higher alcohol content, and so forth.

In general, it is the rise in alcohol content that puts a stop to the fermentation. Therefore, it is recommended to carry out a first racking when a specific gravity reading of 1.020 is obtained. This is the critical moment: the carbon dioxide produced by the yeast is partly imprisoned within the must, inhibiting its activity; also, millions of yeast cells have died and are deposited at the bottom of the carboy. This first racking not only cleans out the accumulated impurities, but oxygenizes the must and releases the excess carbon dioxide, so that the yeast, placed in a more propitious environment for its development, will recommence its alcohol-producing activity until the desired specific gravity measurement is reached.

If by any mischance the fermentation does not start up again, restarter has to be made, that is, yeast has to be cultivated in another medium. The recipe for restarter can be found in Chapter 6 (page 125).

Yeast Nutrients (or Energizer)

To increase the chances of successful fermentation, the elements necessary for the yeast to proliferate must be provided. Besides the glucids that are transformed during the fermentation process, the yeast needs to assimilate mineral substances. These mineral substances are the yeast's food and basic vitamins. Among the mineral elements essential for the yeast cells to multiply are potassium, sodium, calcium, magnesium, iron, phosphorus, sulphur and silicium. Yeast also needs, in much lesser quantities, the following oligo-elements: aluminum, bromine, chromium, copper, lead, manganese and zinc, as well as vitamins B, B1, and C.

Normally, all the minerals and vitamins named above are present in sufficient quantities in the fresh must. However, it

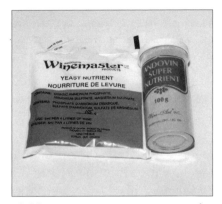

Adding yeast nutrients is strongly recommended when using concentrated and pasteurized musts.

was observed that the addition of phosphate, potassium and magnesium leads to a more rapid, vigorous and successful fermentation.

On the other hand, in the case of concentrated or pasteurized must, a high proportion of the vitamins have been destroyed in the sterilization process, and therefore it is strongly recommended to add yeast nutrients.

Scientific Progress

Over the last fifty years or so, laboratory research has led to enormous gains in the science of oenology. Today, fermentation is no longer a miraculous, hit-or-miss operation. It can now be controlled up to a certain point, and it is a very rare occurence for a winemaker to run up against serious problems during the fermentation stage, for the very good reason that every effort has been made to develop sure-fire, effective yeasts (and to modulate the whole of the fermentation process). The use of selected cultured yeasts has become the *sine qua non* of home winemakers, except for a few die-hard individualists who prefer to remain at the mercy of Mother Nature. In this case, it is far better to trust in science, which has given us a natural product which always works.

Malolactic Bacteria

It is true that the grape harbours bacteria transmitted by the soil, the air, rain, as well as by flies and other insects.

These bacteria are extremely important in the transformation of the must, as well as for the taste of the wine; however, they can also have a hand in spoiling it. Some bacteria are good for wine, while others are ruinous for it.

The bacteria that play an essential positive role in the fermentation process are the malolactic bacteria. They are able to transform malic acid (which naturally has a very acidic taste) into milder lactic acid and volatile carbonic acid. This process, called malolactic fermentation, takes place after the alcoholic (also called primary, or aerobic) fermentation stage. In the warmer wine-producing regions, it begins almost immediately after this stage, while in the cooler production regions of France and Germany, for example, it may only begin six months later, as low winter temperatures prevent malolactic fermentation from occurring.

In earlier times, popular belief attributed qualities to wine that corresponded to the life of plants: it was said that wine underwent a "rising of the sap" in the springtime, which explained the action observed in the vats or the casks. In fact, the higher air temperature induces this fermentation stage. The arrival of spring, particularly in temperate climates, activates the malolactic bacteria which make the wine cloudy and bring about the chemical process described above.

It is important to know that the question of malolactic fermentation need only concern winemakers who are using whole grapes or unsterilized must (fresh refrigerated must). Those who buy pasteurized or concentrated must do not have to worry about it: malolactic fermentation will not take place, because all the bacteria are killed by heat during pasteurization and in the concentration process. Note also that certain musts classified as "natural" or "pure" are actually reconstituted from concentrates[2] and they will not necessarily undergo malolactic fermentation. To know the exact

---

2. See Chapter 5 for types of must.

nature of the must you are buying, you should read the label thoroughly, or ask your retailer about it.

Malolactic fermentation reduces the wine's acidity. Therefore, it is desirable in the case of red wines (naturally acidic and often tannic) as it makes them smoother and more supple, but is less desirable in the case of whites, which may lose some of their crispness and natural liveliness.

The rules are not that simple, however: some white wines, Chardonnay for example, benefit from malolactic fermentation, whereas Riesling and Chenin Blanc lose in the bargain, even though both have a high acidity to begin with.

Thus, malolactic fermentation is an optional process which comes into play in the more complex aspects of winemaking. It can be encouraged or prevented, depending on the final result desired by the winemaker, irrespective of natural acidity rates.

It can be artificially induced by adding malolactic bacteria right after the primary (alcoholic) fermentation stage when the sugar index has greatly decreased, which is the most propitious moment for this type of bacteria to multiply. The wine's temperature must also be warmed to at least 20°C (68°F); if not, malolactic fermentation may stop altogether, or still worse, may occur later on, when the wine is already bottled. The malolactic fermentation stage varies from 2 to 12 weeks.

Inoculation with malolactic bacteria may be necessary when too much metabisulphite has been used after picking the grapes, killing most of the bacteria. This operation must be done with great care, in conditions that are rather too complicated to explain here.

It is possible to know if malolactic fermentation has taken place in a particular wine simply by sending a sample to a laboratory for a chromatography reading of the amounts of malic and lactic acids in the wine. When this analysis is done, the winemaker can take steps to prevent the malolactic bacteria from attacking the tartaric acids later on; when that happens, the wine changes colour, becomes dull-looking, and has a taste making it only fit to throw out. Amateur winemakers who press their own grapes have often suffered the dire consequences of this phenomenon.

The best way to avoid unpleasant surprises is to keep the wine at a temperature of 20° C (68° F) for a period of two or three months. This can be done in two ways: by heating the room to the desired temperature, or by using heating belts around the containers if the wine is stored in a cold room or in a cool basement. At the end of that period, we advise adding a level quarter-teaspoon of potassium metabisulphite which has been dissolved in lukewarm water (or three Campden tablets of sulphur dioxide made from potassium metabisulphite) to every 20 or 23 litres of must [3].

Malolactic fermentation is not recommended for wine to be drunk young. The best way to prevent unwanted malolactic fermentation is to sulphite the wine after the alcoholic fermentation stage. Simply add the same level quarter-teaspoon of potassium metabisulphite previously dissolved in water (or three Campden tablets) to each 20- or 23-litre vat, and the problem will be solved.

The Fermentation of Red Wine

The amateur should be aware that wineries do not proceed in the same manner in the fermentation of red wine as they do in the case of white wine.

When the harvested grapes are rushed to the fermenting rooms, the resident oenologist quickly carries out analyses to verify the quality of the grapes, and makes corrections to the situation by eliminating the fruit considered inappropriate for fermentation and by making chemical and/or physical adjustments.

---

3. For the equivalents in Imperial and U.S. measures, see page 189.

The crushing of the grapes follows, with precautions to avoid grinding up the seeds, which would release too much tannin and oils harmful to the flavour of the wine.

The red grapes are then "destemmed", or detached from their stems. Vintners used to keep part of the stalk to increase the amount of tannin in the wine, but today, the tendency is to eliminate it completely. The consensus is that the tannin contained in the seeds is enough to balance the wine, and that the tannin in the stalk has a rather disagreeable, herbaceous flavour to it.

The industry has developed crusher-destemmers which do both operations at once. The skins are left in contact with

Crushing grapes at a large winery.

the juice and the pulp, to pigment the must to the desired colour. This process also provides a convenient opportunity to inoculate the must with yeasts so that fermentation will begin as soon as possible.

Fermentation is the best way to prevent oxidation. The cardon dioxide that it releases serves as a protective layer against the oxidating effects of the oxygen. Commercial wine production requires huge containers for this process; most industrial wineries opt for either concrete or stainless steel vats, some of which can hold up to 454,000 litres!

The Stages of Fermentation

Primary fermentation takes about 21 days, but after seven to ten days, the wine is siphoned into smaller vats where it will age, protected from oxidation. The method varies according to the quantity of wine being made. Non-*appellation* wines are

Oenologists at work among reservoirs with a capacity of 454,000 litres each (the equivalent of 100,000 gallons, or 600,000 bottles)!

put into stainless steel vats smaller than the fermentors, often with oak chips to create the illusion (*la mode oblige!*) that the wine has been aged in oak barrels. The *appellation mineure* wines are put into authentic oak vats that can hold an astonishing 10,000 litres each (over 2000 gallons!); the *appellations supérieures* have the privilege of going into 225-litre oak casks which, in the case of the best *crus*, are replaced every year to allow the wine to draw as many qualities as possible from the precious wood.

In general, aging in oak casks lasts at least a year. During this time, more wine is added several times to make up for the quantity which has evaporated through the pores of the wood, in a process called "topping up." The wine lost in this natural aging process is called *la part des anges*, or the "angels' share" in French winemaking jargon.

Before bottling, the wine is cleared and stabilized. Clarification methods have evolved considerably since Roman times,

Oak casks of different dimensions.

when a technique called fining was first used. Fining consists of introducing various substances into the wine that will bring the particles that cloud the wine down to the bottom of the barrel. The "glues" that are still used for this today are all natural substances, including defibrinated ox blood, casein, gelatin, egg white and fish glue. This delicate method has been largely abandoned in favour of more expeditious ones, like clearing by centrifugal force. In the wine industry, this operation is done by a centrifuge pump that resembles a juice extractor, but with much more imposing dimensions. The wine is poured into a cylinder, then subjected to rotary action (up to 10,000 rotations/minute) which forces the impurities outward to the walls, which are self-cleaning. Freed from its clouding particles, and also from spent yeast cells, the wine instantly becomes limpid and clear. The centrifuge pump is normally used after primary fermentation has taken place. This prevents the proliferation of harmful bacteria, and during filtration, which is done at a much later stage, the filters will be less clogged up.

Over the last few decades, the practice of filtering wine through pads or cartridges (see Chapter 4) has increasingly come into favour. The wine passing through these types of filtering apparatus is completely cleared of suspended particles or sediment without losing any of its essential qualities.

When these operations are finished, it is the moment for blending the different varietals that the winemaker has available, if he or she chooses to do so. And finally, the wine is ready for bottling, maturing, and marketing. The

Wine grapes ready for crushing.

vintner's job is over, and the wine is now subject to the wine-lover's pleasure!

The Fermentation of White Wine

The fermenting techniques for white wine are almost identical to those for red, with this main difference: the crushing and the pressing operations are done one after the other, so that the stems, seeds, and skins are separated from the must as rapidly as possible. The simple reason for this is that it prevents the wine from being coloured by the skins. The skins of white grapes tend to oxidate very quickly when they are separated from the pulp, and if they are not removed fast enough, they will give a brown colour to the must which will impair the colour of the final product.

Also, to intensify the flavour of white wines, they are subjected to cold fermentation. The temperature of the must is chilled to as low as 8°C (46°F) to slow the fermentation process. This technique is practised on a large scale in the warm wine-producing regions of California, Australia and Italy, to give more flavour to the white wine (for fruity, or pear flavours) by prolonging the transformation of the sugar into alcohol and activating the effects that this longer process has upon the constitution of the must. Cold fermentation methods vary considerably. The most common industrial method is to put the must into huge stainless steel fermentors which have a double wall containing glycol or amonia as a coolant. Another method is to run cold water down the outside surface of the fermentor. In California, cold fermentation is done at temperatures varying between 12°C (54°F) and 14°C (57°F).

Industrial grape-pressing.

Carbonic Maceration

Carbonic maceration [4] is a technique that was first used for red wine in the Beaujolais region many years ago, and which consists in leaving the uncrushed grapes to ferment in a closed vat. The weight of the upper layers of grapes upon those underneath leads to an accumulation of juice at the bottom of the vat, which ferments and produces carbon dioxide. Harking back to ancient times, the sugar is thus transformed into alcohol without adding yeast. Where the hand of modern technology comes in is with the artificial addition of more carbon

---

4. The type of fermentation is also called intracellular fermentation.

Engravings on oak wine casks.

dioxide to ensure that the vat is fully saturated with it, protecting the grapes from oxygen and allowing them to macerate on their own, for seven to twenty-one days. When the gas penetrates the pulp, it brings out the aroma and bouquet, and eliminates excess acidity thanks to the transformation of the malic acid. This allows the wine to be drunk younger, while also giving it a more distinctive flavour.

Once the must has macerated, regular fermentation then occurs. Both the techniques of cold fermentation and carbonic maceration have met with great success. Humble Bordeaux *appellations*, for example, Sirius, Numéro 1 and Michel Lynch, have acquired a much better taste with carbonic maceration, and the sale of these products in North America has shot up. They are best consumed young, however, as the bouquet generated by this kind of fermentation is somewhat volatile and tends to fade with time. In fact, two years after bottling, there is hardly a hint of this distinctive bouquet left.

As for aging and bottling methods, the same rules apply to both red and white wines [5].

---

5. For more details, see the *Bottling and Tasting* volume of the *Encyclopedia of Home Winemaking*.

CHAPTER 3

Biochemical Aspects and Ecological Concerns

or many amateur winemakers, making their own wine is not only a matter of saving money, but also an ecological choice: they feel that the wines sold in stores are not wholly natural products. To a certain extent, they are right, particularly with respect to the cheaper wines available on the market. As these are usually produced in huge quantities, the wine-growers and others involved in the production of these wines do not hesitate to use all of the various chemical means at their disposal to prevent any possiblility of contaminants spoiling their product.

When you make your own wine, you have total control over the production procedure. However, to be able to say that your wine is fully natural, you would have to grow and press your own grapes, as all the musts on the market, either fresh or concentrated, have been treated with chemicals.

A preoccupation with ecological concerns has certain disadvantages: people who avoid the use of any chemicals run the risk of losing their entire production. A few winemakers refuse to add yeast, mistakenly believing that the must will ferment on its own, whereas it has been scientifically proven that pure grape juice does not contain yeast. The absence of yeast is even more undeniable in the case of concentrates: after sterilization, no yeasts or bacteria survive in the must.

Moreover, fanatical environmentally-conscious amateur vintners refuse to use potassium metabisulphite, which they view as a contaminant.

They are wrong in both the preceding cases: the refusal to use yeast in winemaking is an absurdity. Those who stubbornly persist in not using it, and who smirk at other people's incredulous surprise if the must ferments anyway, are probably unaware that this miracle is caused by the yeast cells suspended in the air, invisible but pervasive, that are deposited on the surface of the utensils and containers. These yeasts are so sparse (and more than likely, inappropriate for winemaking) that the magic may not reoccur every year, and without warning, an entire supply of must may be lost in one fell swoop.

This also applies to the refusal to use potassium metabisulphite, a by-product of sulphur dioxide. Making wine at home without it is the equivalent of putting up strawberry jam in unsterilized jars that are not sealed air-tight. Try it, and you can be sure that little round patches of mould will soon appear on the surface of the jam; all of it will have to be thrown out.

Preserving Techniques

Since time immemorial, we have sought to preserve our food in various ways. The practice of boiling food to sterilize it (instigated by Louis Pasteur) is now a common technique. The practice of smoking and drying food to preserve it has a longer history: Amerindian peoples did it long before the Europeans arrived. Yet another method, pickling in brine, was used by our ancestors to preserve meat, fish, and many other foods; when it was time to eat these items, they would be "purged" of their salt. Other liquid solutions are also used to disinfect and protect foods, such as marinating them in vinegar or submerging them in oil (delectable, but watch the cholesterol!).

There are actually hundreds of methods to preserve food nowadays, from vacuum-packing to freezing. The purpose of the majority of these techniques is the same: to prevent the food from coming into direct contact with the air, which always carries bacteria and germs. Exposed to air, the food will inevitably be infested by bacteria and detriorate rapidly. To verify this fact of life, try leaving a steak on the kitchen counter for two weeks, then see (and smell!) the putrid result.

Strangely enough, some wine-lovers are unwilling to admit that wine is a food, and as such, is a potential host to millions of bacteria. If these are allowed to multiply, they will spoil the wine just as they spoil food left at room temperature in the open air: the result may be less disgusting than in meat, but the wine will still be undrinkable, having turned into vinegar, or having acquired a doubtful taste or colour.

In the case of sterilized must, contamination begins at the very instant that the must is re-exposed to the air and put to ferment. It can be said to have "resuscitated," as the organisms in the must will start to teem with life again.

> *You are rashly tempting fate if you give free rein to bacteria that can spoil the wine. If, on the other hand, you are careful and take all the recommended precautions, you will be rewarded by almost guaranteed success.*

Nevertheless, even experienced winemakers may occasionally be negligent, forgetting to wash and sterilize the utensils and instruments that come into contact with the wine. This omission is the equivalent of inoculating the wine with undesirable bacteria. We can never overemphasize the importance of always sanitizing the primary fermentors and the carboys with an appropriate detergent, and of keeping the fermentation locks clean and filled to the recommended level. These procedures should be automatic if we want to produce a decent quality of wine. The inside of the bottles should also be well cleaned (forget about using the dishwasher for this: its hot-water jets hardly ever reach right to the bottom of the bottles).

People who choose not to follow these indispensable rules should be aware that they are drinking the foreign bodies that they have allowed to get into the wine and to grow uncontrolled there. The taste might still be acceptable, but it is by no means certain that the wine will be healthy for drinking.

Chemistry in the Service of Winemaking

The above preamble, we hope, has made it clear that wine must be treated with certain chemical substances if disastrous losses are to be prevented. We mentioned at the beginning of this volume that the Greeks knew how to use sulphur dioxide to prevent oxidation when they made wine. Other chemical substances are also able to do this, and to save or improve upon other desirable qualities that make or break a vintage. In this section, we will introduce the most important ones, to make the reader more familar with them.

Sulphur (Sulphur Dioxide)

Sulphur dioxide is a compound of sulphur, a natural element that constitutes .5 % of the total weight of the Earth; sulphur has so many applications that the amount of it used is a good indicator of a country's economic performance. Sulphur dioxide (SO_2) is created when elemental sulphur (S) is burned in contact with oxygen (O). Sulphur dioxide has several derivatives used in winemaking; these will be discussed in the following subsection and in other sections of this book.

This prickly gas has the particular merit of protecting wine against its most insidious enemy: oxidation. In addition, when it is combined with water (H_2O) in the must or in the wine, it becomes an antiseptic whose qualities have long been appreciated. In fact, sulphur is so effective in winemaking that no better product has ever been found, in spite of decades of intensive research on the subject. Primaricine, Vitamin K2, sorbic acid, ascorbic acid, et alia: none of these substances has proved superior to sulphur in this respect.

> *Sulphur possesses several highly valued properties: it is antifungal (therefore, kills harmful fungus in wine), antibacterial (kills or inhibits bacteria, including the grey mould that appears when the grapes are harvested), antioxidant (prevents the oxidation which makes wine brown and bitter), and antidiastatic (halts the proliferation of enzymes).*

Sulphur not only prevents most of the problems lurking in the organic and inorganic materials of winemaking, but it also invigorates the fermentation process by increasing the alcohol and acid contents of the must, and accentuates the flavour and the colour of the wine.

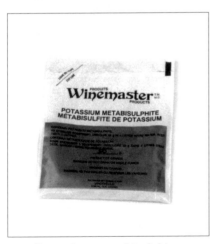

Potassium metabisulphite, a miracle product!

What more could we ask of such a simple, inexpensive substance that, when used with intelligence and moderation, has no harmful effects on our health?

It is easy to understand why vintners prize sulphur dioxide as one of the most valuable chemical compounds in existence, a kind of miraculous preventative medicine in winemaking. 99 % of wine producers use it continually, in the form of compressed gas in tanks (in large-scale production), in wicks (to sterilize oak casks, for example), in liquid form (that is, as an aqueous solution), and finally in the form of granulated salts or crystals.

Potassium Metabisulphate and Other Salts

In general, amateur wine-makers use one of the following sulphur products, in the form of granulated salts (crystals) or tablets: sodium metabisulphite, neutral potassium sulphite, acidic potassium bisulphite, or potassium sulphite. In reality, potassium metabisulphite is used almost systematically because of its high sulphur dioxide content (57%) and also because it is easier to keep fresh than sodium metabisulphite, which starts to smell like lye when it is exposed too long to the air.

Don't forget to fill the fermentation lock with standard potassium metabisulphite solution.

Please note that sodium metabisulphite—contrary to potassium sulphite—may be risky for diabetics. This is why its use is not recommended anymore.

As for Campden tablets, you should only use Campden tablets of potassium metabisulphite: three tablets added three times (3 x 3) per 20 litres [1] or 23 litres of must. Fortunately, Campden sodium metabisulphite tablets have been taken off the market.

Potassium metabisulphite, familiarly called "meta" by home winemakers, is very easy to use. One level quarter-teaspoon of meta crystals is sufficient for 20-30 litres of must.

---

1. For the equivalents in Imperial and U.S. measures, see page 189.

> To administer the precise amount, it is best to use proper measuring spoons. The equivalent of one teaspoon is 5.5 g.: thus, a level quarter-teaspoon is equivalent to 1.4 g., that is, a tiny quantity. This small amount of potassium metabisulphite will produce 31 parts of sulphur dioxide per million (ppm) of wine, far below the present international standard (250 ppm).

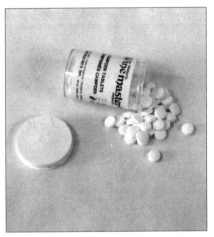

Metabisulphite (Campden) tablets.

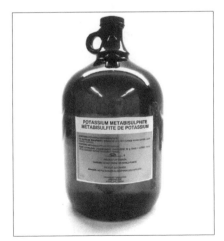

Potassium metabisulphite, or "meta," in a standard 4-litre solution.

We advise you to dilute the metabisulphite in a little lukewarm water before adding it to the must or the wine. The metabisulphite will then dissolve more quickly and effectively, and therefore, if fermentation is still taking place, it will not be absorbed by the enzymes before it has a chance to dissolve throughout the whole contents of the fermentor.

To prepare a standard solution of potassium metabisulphite for antiseptic purposes (to sterilize the utensils and instruments that are used regularly, and for disinfecting the vats, carboys, and other containers), the recipe is simple: dissolve three tablespoons of meta crystals in one gallon (4 litres) of lukewarm water. This stock sulphite solution should be renewed every three months, as its antiseptic powers weaken over time. It is also better to use glass containers, because oxygen eventually penetrates through plastic ones. Labelling the container with the date of mixing is the best way to eliminate any doubts about the solution's effectiveness. Using a vaporizer is a practical and efficient way to sanitize mixing spoons, tubes, and other small instruments and utensils.

A vaporizer is ideal for sanitizing instruments and utensils.

Some people are allergic to sulphur dioxide in the meta, which may cause a skin rash, or choking if the fumes are inhaled. Either way, care should be taken: wear gloves if you have sensitive skin, and if you have any respiratory problems, make sure that you use the potassium metabisulphite in a well-ventilated area.

For people who are strongly allergic to it, substitutes for potassium metabisulphite are available. The Wine-Art company distributes a product called Sterilclean; it comes in liquid form in a little bottle, to be mixed with a gallon (4 litres) of water. It is a quaternary compound, that is, a base rather than an acid (gentler for the skin and milder for breathing). Steril-

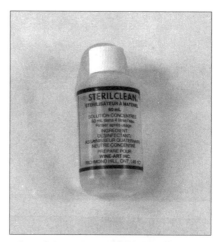

Sterilclean is a mild but effective product for sanitizing equipment.

clean works very well, but after using it, be sure to rinse all the equipment thoroughly, because this product tends to stick to surfaces.

There are new antiseptics sold under the names of Aseptox and Bio-san. These have the same properties as Sterilclean, but it is not necessary to rinse the sterilized equipment as thoroughly after using them.

These substitutes only sterilize the equipment, and not the must itself. Winemakers who are allergic to metabisulphite should nevertheless use sulphur dioxide tablets made from potassium metabisulphite (Campden tablets) to sterilize the must. This process does not expose them to the metabisulphite's effects as much as cleaning the equipment does.

Bio-san is a sanitizing product for winemakers who are allergic to metabisulphite.

Whether or not you are allergic to metabisulphite, you should still use it with moderation. It is easy to know if too much sulphur dioxide is present: its odour (the sulphur smell that is exuded when a match is lit) is strong and disagreeable. Only 11 mg. of it dissolved in one litre of water is enough for the smell to be noticeable. However, the acids contained in wine inhibit the odour of sulphur, and a dosage of up to 35 mg. per litre will not cause any perceptible odour.

Most of the wine-producing countries have imposed norms limiting the excessive use of sulphur dioxide, to protect consumers. These laws are relatively strict today. At the turn of the century, the quantity generally allowed in wine was 500 parts per million (ppm); at the beginning of the 1980s, it was reduced to anywhere between 250 and 300 ppm, depending on the country. An exception is made for dessert wines, which are allowed 500 ppm (because of their high sugar content, more sulphur is required to prevent fermentation from recommencing after bottling). These new standards are mainly the result of intense pressure tactics applied by American groups claiming that specific amounts of sulphur dioxide can be harmful to the health, particularly in the case of asthma-sufferers. This lobby has succeeded in imposing even stricter norms in the United States itself: 160 ppm for red wine, 210 ppm for white wine (which is more susceptible to oxidation and the brown haze known as "casse"), and 400 ppm for dessert wines.

These laws are justified, and should be welcomed. Before this, many people had noticed that they suffered more from headaches after drinking wine in Canada than when they drank a similar amount in Europe. This was because European wines made for export contained much higher proportions of sulphur dioxide than wines for domestic consumption which did not have to travel as far to reach their markets.

Many people have experienced this same type of headache after eating food from buffets and salad bars. In both cases, it is likely that the food was treated with metabisulphite to protect it from oxidation. To give an example, when left in the open air at room temperature, an apple slice that has been sprayed with a metabisulphite solution will only start to turn brown after several hours, whereas an untreated slice will start to rust in less than an hour.

Fortunately, sulphur dioxide possesses two very desirable qualities: it is volatile, and it combines very easily with other chemical bodies present in the must. Very effective in operations that involve manipulating the must (thus exposing it to the air), it evaporates quickly. It spontaneously transforms into SO_3 and into SO_4 to form salts that do not affect the flavour of the wine at all and pose no risk to the health of wine-drinkers, especially when the proper dose has been apportioned.

Another interesting phenomenon concerning sulphur dioxide is that while the volatile (or "free" in chemistry terms) part is evaporating, the part that has combined (to form SO_3 and SO_4) progressively releases SO_2 until an equilibrium is reached between the free and the combined suphur dioxide. It is as if the suphur dioxide were being reserved for the future, thus prolonging its beneficial effects on the must or wine.

This said, the metabisulphite never totally disappears from the must. Therefore, it is strongly recommended not to use an excessive amount of it (more than the legal norm), especially as the proportion of free sulphur dioxide increases sharply (from 55% to 66%) when another equivalent dose is added.

> *Therefore, it is recommended to sulphite the must three times, including at the bottling stage, with one level quarter-teaspoon of meta (or three Campden tablets) every time, if the norms are to be observed. In the case of fresh red must, the same number of doses of metabisulphite are recommended; however the doses should be given at slightly different stages to encourage malolactic fermentation* [2].

The threefold addition of the recommended dose of metabisulphite will give your wine a total of approximately 150 ppm of SO_2, which is considerably less than the allowed norm (250-300 ppm) in most of the world.

> *You can quite confidently add metabisulphite in the recommended doses. Your wine will then be safe for consumption and protected from contamination. If, on the other hand, you refuse to do it, especially during the last racking and the bottling stage, you are taking grave and unnecessary risks.*
> *If you are using concentrated, semi-concentrated, or sterilized must, you can ignore the above suggestions because*

---

2. See Chapters 2 and 6.

metabisulphite is usually already included in the packets of additives provided by the producers.

Amateurs who make large quantities of wine will benefit from using Tannisol tablets. These are large tablets, about 2.5 cm. (1 inch) in diametre and weighing almost 10 g., consisting of 95 % potassium metabisulphite, 3 % ascorbic acid (Vitamin C), and 2 % tannin. One tablet dissolved in 100 litres of must releases about 30 ppm of free sulphur dioxide. Tannisol can also be used, if this is desired, in 20-litre or 23-litre carboys: each tablet should be split into quarters. A quarter of a Tannisol tablet, when dissolved, releases the same amount of free SO_2 (that is, 30 ppm) as one quarter-teaspoon of meta.

It is inside the bottles that there is the highest possiblility of finding excessive sulphur, especially when the wine is drunk young. Therefore, particular care must be taken before bottling not to add too much sanitizing product. The best procedure is either to fill the bottle with standard metabisulphite solution, swirl it around thoroughly and drain it, or to sulphite it with a special apparatus [3] . In both cases, the bottles should be placed with their necks downward so that as much of the solution as possible will drain out of them.

To know more about sulphur use for bottling, see *Bottling and Tasting*, Volume 2 of *The Encyclopedia of Home Winemaking*.

Before we move on to the next subject, we should mention that there are home kits to measure the amount of SO_2 in wine; they cost about $20 Cdn. The instructions for using the kit appear in Chapter 7.

Detergents

We reiterate, and cannot overemphasize that the success or failure of your wine depends largely on the cleanliness of

---

3. See Chapter 4.

your equipment. It is not an exaggeration to say that extreme prudence must be the rule in this aspect. Every time the must is handled, the instruments used should be sprayed with standard meta solution to prevent contamination. All the containers which will hold the must or the wine have to be meticulously cleaned: the primary fermentors (tubs, pails, buckets, or vats), the carboys or demi-johns, the bottles, etc. As you probably know, plastic containers tend to carry bacteria much more easily than glass ones. In fact, plastic is infinitely less resistant than glass; every scratch on the inside of a plastic pail becomes a potential nest for bacteria.

Detergent for cleaning vats, carboys, and other instruments.

> *Therefore, the primary fermentors should be replaced at least every three years to avoid irreparable losses. We also suggest a thorough yearly clean-up of the room or area where the wine is made (using disinfectants like Javex or Lysol). Bacteria (as well as yeasts, moreover) travel fast and deposit themselves everywhere.*

Winemaking stores sell special detergents, or sanitizers (most are chlorine-based, in the form of pink powder), which thoroughly clean the fermentors, lifting off any deposit that may coat them, and disinfecting them. There are several products on the market, and almost all of them are effective. They contain more chlorine than ordinary cleansers; at the same time, the fact that they contain very little potash cuts down on rinsing time.

No matter which cleansers are used, you should rinse the instruments or containers with spring water or distilled water to remove any residual sanitizing product. This point is essential when carboys and bottles are washed with an antiseptic detergent: if they aren't rinsed properly, it is more than likely that the wine's taste will remind you of the smell of lye.

The Antioxidants

Must has to be protected from bacteria, but also against the effects of oxidation. If the must has too much contact with the air, it will oxidate rapidly, and the future wine will be vinegar instead!

Certain substances act as antioxidants: they arrest the harmful action of oxidation. These include ascorbic acid (Vitamin C) and sodium erythorbate.

Each of these two substances acts in synergy; along with the potassium metabisulphite, their combined effects produce a very high degree of antioxidant power, although only a tiny quantity of each of them is required. For example, 14 g. (5 oz.) of sodium erythorbate is enough to protect 450 litres (100 gallons) of wine!

As for Vitamin C (ascorbic acid), it is used both as an antioxidant and for improving the wine. In fact, one level quarter-teaspoon of it, dissolved in a 20-litre or 23-litre carboy before bottling, will give the wine greater freshness, colour, and aroma. But let us emphasize that neither of these products is antiseptic and therefore cannot replace metabisulphite for that purpose.

You should also consult your home wine equipment retailer if you are faced with particularly challenging oxidation problems.

Oxido-Reduction

As contradictory as it may seem, oxygen, the sworn enemy of wine in many circumstances, is an important element in the maturation of process. In the evolution of winemaking, the phenomenon of reduction has come to be viewed as an essential biochemical contribution in the development of flavour.

Let us explain. Even though the must should never be left in the open air, it does enter into contact with the air at least twice, and more likely three, four, or five times during the vinification process: right before the alcoholic, or primary fermentation stage, right before secondary fermentation and during subsequent racking, and finally, when the wine is bottled. Thus, the wine will have been aerated, or oxidized, several times, albeit for very brief periods.

An explanation of the phenomenon of oxido-reduction allows us to understand what happens when the must comes into contact with oxygen. The must reacts spontaneously with the small quantity of oxygen which is trapped inside the closed carboy or bottles. The electrons released by the oxygen are immediately captured by the must and reduced (or absorbed) slowly by it, until a new balance is attained in the must, or wine. The oxidizing product (the air) is in a struggle with the reducing agent (the must or wine), and the reaction constitutes a kind of defence

Musts in fermentation. The white wine has a heating belt.

mechanism. Reduction is necessary to the maturation process because this additional chemical action contributes substantially to bringing about a new equilibrium in the wine.

Therefore, we recommend a waiting period before drinking the new vintage once it is bottled: the reduction phenomenon does not produce its beneficial effects until a few weeks have passed (this period varies according to the quality of the wine and its tannins). In general, one should wait at least a month, and preferably three or four months, before drinking the wine.

A redox potential table allows the winemaker to compare the quantity of oxygen that has been reduced by the must to the ideal reduction potential. This analysis of the reduction phenomenon is very useful when blending different varietals. A perfectly balanced wine can be achieved by calculating how much of each varietal should be used, according to this table. Of course, these operations are only carried out by the makers of the finest wines.

Acids

If there is one element of paramount importance in the constitution of a wine, it is undoubtedly its acidity rate. The amateur vintner should ask the winemaking retailer if it will be necessary to balance the wine that he or she is going to make. Winemakers who press their own grapes are practically obliged to carry out their own tests to determine the acidity levels of the must. Then, they should modify it (if indicated) to harmonize with the accepted norms. The same obligatory testing is required for concentrated musts that are not already balanced (although these are becoming harder to find).

Usually, the purchaser of a concentrate kit, sterilized must, or fresh refrigerated must does not have to worry about balancing the acidity rate: these musts are already balanced and ready to ferment.

Balancing the acidity rate is all the more important because acidity varies according to the geographical area where the grapes are grown and the climatic conditions that prevail as they ripen. As we mentioned in Chapter 1, warmer climates produce grapes with lower acidity rates, while in cooler wine-producing regions, the acidity rates tend to be higher. On the other hand, the grapes grown in warm regions contain more sugar, which explains why the wines made from them have a very high alcohol content: 14% or even 15% (28° - 30° Proof).

Balancing the acidity rate in wine is necessary for several reasons, with flavour considerations not surprisingly at the top of the list. An overly acidic wine has a disagreeable taste; the acid brings on excessive salivation and is needlessly aggressive to the palate. On the other hand, a wine with a very low acidity rate is flat and flavourless.

Another essential reason for striving to achieve a good acid balance is that it protects the wine against bacteria, particularly vinegar bacteria, as well as from oxidation and undesirable colour changes. Finally, correcting the acidity helps keep the wine crisp.

The acidity rate can be measured in two ways: either in terms of power (the strength of the acids), or as a relative quantity. Its power is measured on a pH scale (hydrogen-ion potential) which determines the effective rate of active acidity in the wine. The lower the pH level, the higher the acidity rate. Water, for example, is neutral, and its pH level is 7, whereas a wine with a balanced acidity will have a pH level of 3.1 to 3.5. A wine with a high acidity level has a lemony bite to it; a wine with a low acid content is flat. With this knowledge and the ability to measure the acidity, appropriate adjustments can be made according to the desired final result.

To go about it, a simple kit is available for determining the hydrogen-ion concentration in the wine. It is composed of little strips of reagent paper (called pH paper), and a series of colour grades representing different pH levels. The strips, dipped into the wine, will take on the colour corresponding to the particular pH level represented in the table. The pH level of the must or the wine can thus be known to an approximate degree.

There are, of course, more accurate electronic instruments to measure pH levels. The prices of these pH-meters differ widely (from $35 to $3000 Cdn!), but they are very easy to use and give a much

A pH-meter.

more precise reading than is possible with the pH papers. They are used mostly by commercial wineries, and by those people who aim for absolute control over their winemaking process.

However, as far as acidity is concerned, the taste of the wine is not only influenced by its concentration in hydrogen ions, but also by the totality of the acids present in it. By carrying out an acidimetric analysis of the wine, it is possible to obtain an accurate reading of the acids contained in it (pH level and quantity of acids).

To obtain a complete reading of the acidity of the wine, it is therefore necessary to also do an acidity reading in terms of quantities: here, the quantity of acid is measured in grams per litre. Red wine usually contains between five and six grams of acid per litre. For this calculation as well, there exists an acid titration kit to take these measurements. The directions are generally quite clear, and involve neutralizing the acid in a wine sample of known volume, using a measured solution; then, using a simple formula, the total quantity of acid contained in the sample can be calculated.

The problem with acidity is that you may have a desirable acidity rate, but an insufficient pH level, because not all acids have the same properties: there can be different pH levels for two identical quantities of acid. For example, the pH level of tartaric acid is higher than that of citric acid; therefore, if you balance your acidity rate with citric acid, you will obtain a desirable acidity balance (proportionally), but your pH level may be inadequate. Another example will illustrate this difference: a metal immersed in hydrochloric acid will be strongly attacked by the acid, whereas the same metal immersed in the same amount of citric acid will not be. The explanation lies in the fact that the respective pH levels of the two acids are very different indeed, with the result that hydrochloric acid is much stronger than citric acid.

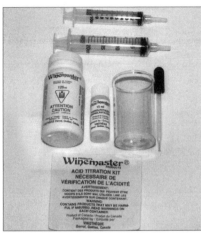

A titration kit for measuring acidity in wine.

As we mentioned earlier, wine contains three major acids in variable proportions: tartaric acid, citric acid, and malic acid. Tartaric acid has a mucher higher pH level than the other two; therefore, it is quite a complex operation to correct the acidity while respecting the proportions which occur naturally in the wine and which give it its characteristic flavour and aroma. There are acid blends on the market which take this natural balance into account: the relative proportions of the acids are different according to the type of

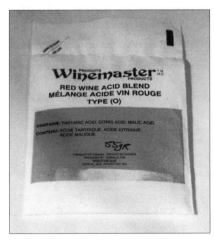

An acid blend used to balance the wine.

wine, red or white. It is a good idea to ask your winemaking retailer for advice about these crucial details, especially because a deficiency may be present in only one of the acids that are contained in the wine.

When making wine from fresh refrigerated must or from whole grapes, it is recommended to use tartaric acid by itself, as the citric acid contained in acid blends can be attacked and transformed by the bacteria contained in the fresh must.

It is also possible to decrease the acidity of your wine. The simplest way of doing this is to blend an overly acidic wine with a less acidic one. If this operation is not possible, another recommended method is to add potassium carbonate or calcium carbonate (chalk) to the must; your retailer will likely stock them. Note however, that the acidity rate cannot be lowered to less than 1.5 or 2 grams per litre without sacrificing the better part of the wine's flavour and bouquet.

You have probably concluded by now that it is less risky and more convenient to buy a must that has already been acid-balanced. Ordinarily, you should not have to deal with correcting the acid balance. However, some home winemakers prefer to do their own analyses and improvements of the acidity rates of their musts. This is why we have provided the above explanation.

Clarifiers

Most amateur winemakers make it a point of honour to serve their friends a clear, limpid wine; to them, it is evidence of the wine's success.

We have seen in the fermentation process that the action of the yeast makes the must undergo a radical transformation during which it changes into wine. This very complex process completely clouds the fermented must. After ten days, a first racking will restart fermentation by removing most of the dead yeasts cells, by releasing the excess carbon dioxide gas, and finally, by oxygenizing the must.

Three weeks later, the essential part of the fermentation process will have taken place. The yeast cells gradually die. The particles suspended in the must slowly drift down to the bottom of the carboy. The wine then enters a calmer phase during which it clears. The clearing phenomenon takes several weeks, even months; it is said that for the wine to clear completely, it takes up to six months.

It may happen that the wine is not clear even after six months. To achieve a completely clear wine, the winemaker is offered two solutions, filtering the wine[4], or fining it with clarifying products. In fact, both methods may be used to obtain even more satisfactory results.

Winemakers who like concentrates which guarantee fast results (for example, the 28-day kit) will have to use clarifying and stabilizing products if they want to drink their wine young.

There is no risk in using clarifying products. Generally speaking, they are natural substances which, in correct doses, are in no way harmful to the health.

Bentonite

Discovered in Fort Benton, U.S.A., bentonite is found in large quantities in Wyoming. It is a clay dust made up of aluminum oxides and silicone, which have properties capable of bringing the solids suspended in the wine down to the bottom of the carboy. To explain this fining process in more precise terms, the bentonite contains negative ions which bind with the positively-charged particles suspended in the must. Once the binding has occurred, the transformed solids sink to the bottom of the carboy because the bentonite has made them heavier than the surrounding liquid.

---

4. See Chapter 4.

The directions for use are simple: mix the required dose of bentonite with water before adding it to the must. Bentonite tends to lump, and must be mixed very thoroughly; therefore, we suggest using a covered container to shake it up well. Bentonite never completely dissolves in water; see Chapter 7 for another effective way of mixing bentonite.

> *The effectiveness of bentonite as a clarifying agent is indisputable. In a few days, the wine becomes crystal-clear. However, this lovely clarity comes with a price: bentonite also takes away from the wine's complexity, and diminishes its bouquet by about 15%. Bentonite may also give the wine an earthy taste.*

Isinglass

Isinglass is a type of gelatin which has long been used as a natural coagulant to clear wine. It is extracted from the internal membrane of the air bladder[5] of the sturgeon. It is sold in the form of sheets ("leaf isinglass"), ribbons, or "pipe isinglass", and has several uses. In the wine industry, it is used for clearing purposes. The membrane is cut up into tiny pieces and dissolved in cold water (a minute quantity

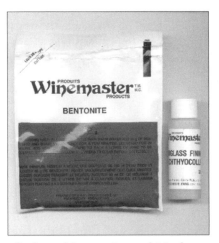

Packaged bentonite and isinglass.

---

5. The air bladder, or swimming bladder, is a membranous sack which is connected to the oesophagus of the fish and regulates its equilibrium in the water by filling and emptying itself of gas. We don't know whose idea it was to use this substance for clearing wine, but this is certainly a fascinating example of human ingenuity!

of hydrochloric acid will facilitate dissolution). The result is a viscous jelly that can be converted into powder or kept as is.

The advantage of using isinglass in powder form is that it is easier to measure out an exact quantity; one can simply take the required proportion and reconstitute the isinglass. The process that takes place in the wine is the reverse of what happens with bentonite: here, the positive ions of the isinglass combine with the negatively-charged solids in the wine and bring them down to the bottom of the carboy, clearing the liquid. There is practically no effect upon the quality of the wine in the case of isinglass. The complementarity of the chemical actions of bentonite and isinglass is the reason that they are often used together to achieve a high degree of clearness.

We suggest the use of powdered isinglass because isinglass in jelly form gradually loses its inherent characteristics when it is placed in a solution, becoming a simple gelatin. In its gelatinous state, it is much less effective than in its natural state.

Kielselsol (Claro K.C.)

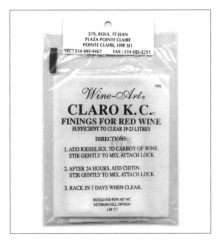

Kielselsol, sold under the brand name Claro K.C.

Kielselsol is a silica gel (SiO_2). This product was developed by Bayer, the German pharmaceutical company, in the 1940s. The association of silica and gelatin is the equivalent of the bentonite-isinglass combination. To use it, the silica must be diluted 24 hours before adding the gelatine. Kielselsol is a extremely effective product, particularly in the case of wines that do not contain much tannin (a characteristic of wines made from concentrated, sterilized, and fresh musts). As tannin is a natural clarifier of wine, it is understandable that it is sometimes necessary to use clarifying products when using those musts. The reason that concentrated, sterilized, and fresh refrigerated musts are not required to contain a lot of tannin is simply that it is presumed that the wines made from them will be drunk young, and not aged in cellars for decades like the great Burgundies and Bordeaux, which are necessarily high in tannins.

Kielselsol is marketed by the Wine-Art company under the name of Claro K.C. Wine-Art has created two specific products, one for red wines and the other for white.

Other Clarifiers

There are other clarifying products based on albumen (egg white), casein, and defibrinated ox blood. We suggest that you consult your winemaking retailer to know which product is best suited for your purposes. Generally speaking, we would recommend those that we have described above, that is, bentonite, isinglass and Kielselsol.

Pectinase (Pectic Enzymes)

It is not always easy to determine the cause of the clouding of wine.

A slight milkiness may be due to an excess of pectin when elderberries or other fruit-based flavours are added to the wine. A simple test can determine whether pectin is the culprit: mix one part of the clouded wine with four

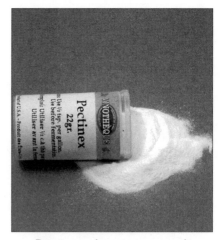

Pectinase (pectic enzymes) in powder form.

parts alcohol. If pectin is the cause of the clouding, it will be deposited at the bottom of the container in the form of gelatinous clots and strings. This operation takes up to one hour to show a definite result.

If the test is conclusive, the excess pectin can be eliminated by using pectinase, an enzyme which absorbs the pectin and thus clears the wine.

Pectinase is generally sold as a white powder, and is used in minute quantities. The directions provided by the maker must be followed to the letter.

Stabilizers

Stabilizing the wine at one point or another is recommended. Stabilizing the wine does not mean killing all the life in the bottle, as some people believe; rather, it simply prevents the possibility that refermentation will occur after bottling. In fact, it is vastly preferable that the wine continue to be alive as it matures, until it is drunk. However, winemakers should be aware that even after a successful fermentation, there is still residual sugar in the wine that has the potential to turn into alcohol and carbon dioxide at any given moment. The amount of residual sugar is estimated at between one quarter and one half of a percentage point in dry wine, and up to two percent in sweet wine.

Therefore, if nothing is done to inhibit yeast action, the risk of refermentation exists. If this occurs, in the best of cases, the wine will become semi-sparkling, and in the worst case, it will be lost if the cork shoots out during the maturation stage.

There are several stabilization methods. Some of these are not accessible to home winemakers, for example, the use of a centrifuge machine which expels all the yeast that might become active again inside the bottles. Some commercial wineries carry out a sterilizing filtration process which blocks the passage of the still-active yeast and bacteria in the cleared wine.

It is true that the addition of potassium metabisulphite (meta) inhibits fermentation, but the quantities that we have recommended to home wine-makers are not sufficient to prevent refermentation after bottling.

Potassium sorbate.

For this, it is better to use potassium sorbate, a derivative of sorbic acid. Potassium sorbate has been officially declared non-toxic, non-carcinogenic, and otherwise absolutely harmless to the health.[6] This is all the more certain because the quantities of it required for stabilizing wine are minuscule compared with the amounts of it used in other food products (particularly in the manufacture of cookies and cakes).

A dose of two teaspoons of potassium sorbate are required for 20 or 23 litres of wine. You should know, however, that potassium sorbate may spoil the wine if it has undergone malolactic fermentation, giving it a geranium odour which renders it undrinkable. This warning therefore applies only in the case of wines made from fresh must or from whole grapes [7]. Wines made from concentrated, semi-concentrated, or sterilized must do not undergo malolactic fermentation.

---

6. Potassium sorbate was officially exonerated from having any known cancer-causing properties at the conclusion of 35 years of testing different products that contained it.

7. As we have explained, malolactic fermentation only occurs in non-sterilized must. It cannot take place in concentrated and semi-concentrated musts, and in sterilized juice, because the sterilization process kills the malolactic bacteria.

In the case of wine made from fresh must or pressed grapes, we suggest that you proceed in the following manner: add one level quarter-teaspoon of meta crystals (dissolved in luke-warm water) to 20 or 23 litres of must, then wait three days before stabilizing the wine with potassium sorbate. In this way, the malolactic bacteria which can cause the disagree-able geranium odour will be suppressed or destroyed.

To obtain infallible results, we strongly recommend that the wine contain sufficient potassium metabisulphite, that is, 30 ppm of free sulphur dioxide (SO_2) at the time of bottling (see Chapter 6 on this subject).

The different products described in this chapter will appear in other parts of this book, particularly in the central section on the winemaking process. All of them are used frequently in winemaking at home as well as in the industry. Therefore, it is important to be familiar with their composition and their properties, the precautions that should be taken when using them, and the cases in which they are counter-indicated.

CHAPTER 4

The Basic Equipment and How to Use It

To make wine with concentrated, semi-concentrated, pasteurized, or fresh must, or from whole grapes, a certain number of containers, utensils, and instruments are essential. The material required is less expensive than it might seem at first glance. With a budget of only about $55 Cdn., it is possible to be reasonably well-equipped to make good wine. This is not very much to pay considering that it will allow you to produce wine for about $2 Cdn. per bottle (on the average, taking into account the varying prices of the different qualities of must). Also, you will use this equipment again and again. Of course, as your skill and your desire to reach greater heights in this art grow, you may want to invest in more elaborate, expensive equipment.

If you are a beginner, it is wise to proceed with prudence. Luckily, most retailers of must offer their new customers complete kits at varying prices, depending on the quality of the equipment provided. To give an example, a glass carboy costs more than a plastic fermentor. It is also possible to choose from among several types of hydrometers, some more expensive than others. Generally speaking, the retailers of musts and winemaking equipment are honest with their customers in the matter of prices, as they quite naturally want to cultivate long-term relationships with them.

This chapter describes the most important recipients, utensils, and instruments needed for making wine at home.

The Primary Fermentor

The primary fermentor, usually a pail or bucket, must prevent the must from overflowing. This container must have a large opening to allow the escape of the large quantity of carbon dioxide gas that is released during the first few days of fermentation (and also to allow convenient cleaning). Besides this, to stop the must from overflowing, the capacity of the primary fermentor must be greater than the volume of the must put into it to ferment. There should be at least 10 centimetres (4 inches) left at the top to contain the froth formed by the fermenting must.

Therefore, we suggest a 30-litre container to serve as a primary fermentor for each 23 litres of must, the standard quantity of many of the packaged musts on the market. This quantity of must will yield approximately 30 bottles of wine! The primary fermentor is usually a plastic tub or pail. You will also need plastic sheeting to cover the fermentor. To secure the cover safely, we suggest tying it around with a cord attached to an elastic band at both ends. As an alternative, giant-sized elastic bands (15 cm. or 6 in. long when in repose), are sold in office equipment and stationery stores.

Some primary fermentors have their own lids with a place to install a bung. Although these lids require additional handling, this type of fermentor is becoming increasingly popular because it protects the must from bacteria from outside sources better than other kinds of fermentors. It also offers better protection against any domestic animals (especially those curious cats!) who might end up swimming in the must, ruining five gallons of wine in a few seconds!

If you choose to use a plastic pail that is not white, make sure it is marked "food grade quality", or "for alimentary use." Coloured pails that do not carry this label should never be used: they may contain a high degree of lead and are therefore toxic. They can also spoil the wine's flavour.

Primary fermentors with built-in taps near their base are sold in winemaking supply stores; we do not recommend their use, mainly because the addition of the tap increases the likelihood of contamination by bacteria. If you do own one of these primary fermentors, ask your retailer about the proper way of sanitizing it thoroughly.

Experienced and provident winemakers often prefer to use glass containers, even for the primary fermentation stage.

A primary fermentor.

In this case, care should be taken to choose the right size: 20 litres of must can be fermented in a 23-litre carboy, and 23 litres in a 28-litre carboy. In this way, a bung can be fitted into the neck without any risk of overflow. This method is safe and very effective. However, glass carboys require the same amount of attention as the other types of fermentors do (that is, racking when the density goes down to 1.020 or less). Using glass carboys for the primary fermentation stage is inevitably more expensive than using plastic containers; therefore, we only recommend it for people who have been making wine for quite a long time.

The Secondary Fermentor

For the secondary fermentation stage and for aging in bulk (*cuvaison*), glass or plastic carboys are generally used. The plastic carboys come in a standard 23-litre format and are made of polyethylene, or polypropylene, which are inert plastics. Thus, no reaction occurs between the material and the wine. They are about five kilograms (11 lbs.) lighter than glass carboys, which makes them easier to handle. Their main disadvantage with respect to glass carboys is that they are relatively opaque, and consequently, it is more difficult to verify the clarity of the wine, or to see if any fermentation is taking place. An even more important factor to consider is that plastic containers cannot be used for wine that is meant to age for more than three months before bottling, as they are not impermeable to air. The oxygen can penetrate the plastic material and oxidate the wine if it is left that long. Also, as we mentioned earlier, the inner walls of plastic fermentors, not being as smooth or as resistant as glass, are more likely to harbour bacteria that may spoil the wine.

We warn you against using the clear plastic bottles that hold commercial brands of mineral water, spring water, or distilled water. The material of these containers may start to disintegrate due to the effect of the alcohol, and thus be harmful to the health. The labels on these containers, moreover, normally carry a clear warning against this kind of use.

Thus, glass is definitely preferable for the secondary fermentation stage, particularly if you intend to keep your wine for a considerable period in the carboy for aging in bulk. This said, it is better to choose a container with vertical seams (there are usually four of them from the neck to the base). These carboys are less likely to split open than the ones that have a (not very visible) manufacturing seam at the base. The latter type is susceptible to temperature variations, and can break open during use.

Carboys or secondary fermentors are available in several different sizes. The biggest ones can hold 28 litres, but they also come in smaller sizes, with capacities of 4 litres, 11.5 litres, 15 litres, 18 litres, 19 litres, 20 litres, and 23 litres.

Most home winemakers use the 20- or the 23-litre carboys, simply because these volumes correspond to the standard quantities of must commonly sold.

Carboys for secondary fermentation and bulk aging.

The debutant winemaker should restrain his or her enthusiasm with regard to size: consider that these mega-bottles have to be manipulated at least two or three times during the winemaking process, and lifting a full 54-litre demi-john is hardly the same thing as lifting a magnum (1.5 litre) of Champagne!

Caution! Do not wash out glass or plastic carboys with hot water.

Finally, don't be shocked if you discover that your carboys do not hold exactly the amount indicated. The difference may be one, or even two litres (about half a gallon). However, perfection is rare in this world! You should get used to the little surprises that come up in this pastime, and learn to cheerfully adapt in consequence. Thus, be prepared to discover, when you are racking your wine from one container to another, that you don't have quite enough to reach the desired level.

Demi-johns, or *dames-jeannes.*

Demi-johns, or *dames-jeannes*, are available in several sizes. They are pear-shaped glass bottles, and have either a protective plastic grid or a wicker covering complete with handles. They are actually more practical than plain carboys, but are less appreciated by some amateur winemakers because they are more fragile. They are made of blown glass and therefore, are slightly irregular: some parts may be thinner than others, which makes them more susceptible to breaking than carboys. They also take longer to clean, as it is necessary to remove and replace their protective coverings. However, the covering is not only useful for protecting the glass: it also keeps light from affecting the colour of the wine. Winemakers who appreciate demi-john bottles should therefore leave them the way they were when they were bought; otherwise, they might just as well use conventional carboys instead.

A start-up kit: a primary fermentor, a glass carboy, rigid and flexible tubing, a hydrometer, a fermentation lock and bung, and a stirring spoon.

Barrels or Casks

Of course, it is an advantage to use wooden barrels for aging your own wine: the wine will acquire a better bouquet and finish. However, we only recommend it for experienced winemakers, as it increases the risk of spoiling the wine by contamination. Barrels are generally used for red wine, although Chardonnay and certain other white wines will profit from maturing in barrels as well.

Only barrels appropriate for winemaking should be used. Used barrels should be avoided, particularly if they have been allowed to dry out; it is impossible to safely sanitize a barrel once the staves have dried out and drawn apart.

New barrels for winemaking are expensive; gone are the days when used barrels were completely reconditioned by coopers. Oak barrels from France which have been especially prepared by being exposed to the elements for a period up to ten years are the best, but even North American white oak casks are excellent.

Careful preparations are required before transferring the wine to the barrel. The barrel must be well-soaked with water containing sulphite. You should definitely consult your retailer before embarking on this delicate aspect of winemaking. We will go into greater detail about barrels in the second volume of *The Encyclopedia of Home Winemaking*, entitled *Bottling and Tasting*.

Other Utensils

There are a few other essential utensils and instruments required in home winemaking. Most of them are quite inexpensive. We will describe them briefly here.

The Stirring Spoon

This long plastic spoon usually has two ends, one that is small enough to pass through the neck of the carboy, and the other broader, for stirring the must in the primary fermentor. It has several uses.

Tubes and Other Instruments Needed for Racking

The safest way to transfer wine from one container to another is by siphoning it. Any other method may cause an unwanted spillage of wine.

For siphoning wine, you will need:

a) A flexible plastic tube or hose, at least 2 metres (6 ft.) long.

b) A rigid tube, usually called a J-tube, at least 10 cm. (4 in.) longer than the height of your carboy. This tube is bent

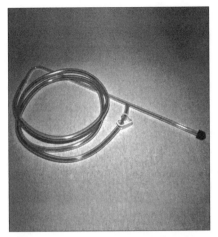

Rigid tube joined to the flexible siphon hose.

at both ends, at an acute angle at the top and in a J-curve at the bottom. It is placed into the full primary fermentor with the curved end touching the bottom; the tube end will therefore be a little above the bottom and will not draw in the sediment.

Another version of the rigid tube is fitted with a special cap, or anti-sediment tip, which prevents the sediment from entering when the wine is siphoned.

The purpose of the acute-angled bend at the top end of the J-tube is simply to prevent the flexible tube from bending over on itself and blocking the flow of the wine as it is drawn out into the new recipient.

A hook prevents the rigid tube from falling off the carboy or the fermentor.

c) A clamp to pinch the siphon tube closed at the receiving end; this is an easy way to stop the flow if the recipient appears about to overflow, or for any other reason.

d) A racking tube clip, or hook, is also useful: with the rigid tube pushed through it, it is hooked onto the neck of the carboy, or over the rim of the primary fermentor. In this way, the siphon tube cannot suddenly fall away from the carboy or the fermentor because of a false move on the part of the winemaker.

Racking by siphoning is a fairly easy operation. Simply position the two containers at different heights, the full one higher than the empty one. Ideally, the bottom of the full container should be level with, or a little bit higher than the neck of the carboy to be filled. When the recipients are in the proper position (with newspapers on the floor in case of spills), place the rigid J-tube inside the full fermentor, stretch out the flexible hose that is attached to the acute-angle end at the top, then suck until the wine has flowed into at least two-thirds of the total length of the siphon hose. Pinch the hose closed with your fingers or with the clamp, then put the unattached end into the empty recipient and release your fingers or the clamp. The pressure created by the difference between the levels will bring all the wine from the elevated fermentor into the lower-placed carboy.

This simple procedure can be enjoyable, unless frequent splashings end up staining your favourite carpet or your natural wood flooring. To be absolutely safe, it is better to put plastic sheeting under the old newspapers.

The Auto-Siphon

Winemakers who dislike swallowing any metabisulphite solution or must at the beginning of the racking process can use the Auto-Siphon. This instrument is a cylinder into which is inserted a rigid tube with an acute-angle bend at the top. When using it, make sure the tube reaches to the bottom of the cylinder. Submerge the Auto-Siphon into the liquid to be racked; pump the rigid tube up and down about 15 cm. (6 in.) until the wine flows into the hose, and into the secondary recipient. This instrument works well and is highly appreciated by many home winemakers.

The Fermentation Lock

The fermentation lock, also called airlock, has long since replaced, in the name of superior efficiency, the earlier practice of adding a layer of edible oil on top of the wine after siphoning it into the secondary fermentor, or carboy. The purpose of the oil, and of the fermentation lock, is to protect the wine from contact with the air while still allowing the carbon dioxide gas to escape. To accomplish this, a simple solution was found: the installment of a low-pressure barrier between the wine in the carboy and the outside air.

There presently are two types of fermentation lock available. The first one, made of plastic, has a characteristic shape: a transparent tube curved in the form of an S placed horizontally. The bottom extremity of the tube passes through a stopper, usually a rubber bung, which fits into the neck of the carboy. The lock has two enlargements, or wells, half way up two sides of the S. Standard metabisulphite solution is poured into it until it reaches the half-way mark in both of the wells. The gas produced by the slow secondary fermentation in the carboy exerts gradual pressure on the metabisulphite solution, pushing it past the lowest part of the loop of the S. As soon as that point is reached, the excess gas can escape as bubbles rising through the metabisulphite solution into the open air beyond it. Freed from the pressure, the solution returns to its original level, completely protecting the wine from exposure to the air.

It may happen, however, that air is drawn towards the inside of the lock; this is usually due to a rapid change in temperature. In fact, the system works in both directions, even if it may be disastrous for air to get into the must.

Thus, the fermentation lock is both a simple and ingenious invention which works well as long as the level of liquid is monitored at regular intervals, as any liquid will eventually evaporate.

Watching the level attentively will prevent this from happening.

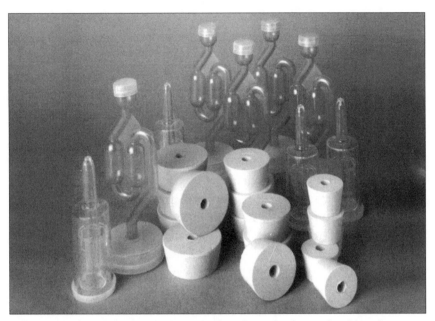

S-shaped fermentation locks, cylindrical cap locks, and rubber bungs.

The other type of fermentation lock is based on the same principle. It is a capped clear plastic cylinder which fits into the neck of the carboy. Attached inside it (vertically) is a smaller cylinder, or rigid tube, with openings at both the top and bottom; the top of the tube is at a level one-third of the way down from the top of the larger cylinder. The tube continues through the bottom of the bung, or stopper, reaching down into the secondary fermentor (but above the suface of the wine). The metabisulphite solution is poured inside the main cylinder of the lock to just below the top opening of the tube, which is covered by a moveable inverted cap, allowing the gases to escape while preventing the air from penetrating the carboy. As long as it is working properly, the result is the same as with the first type of lock, that is, the wine is never in contact with the air, and is therefore protected from bacteria that might spoil it.

At the present time, the cylindrical fermentation lock is becoming the norm and is sold more frequently. Nevertheless, the S-shaped lock has certain advantages over the cylindrical type, even if it is more difficult to clean if a mixture of wine and metabisulphite occurs; its main advantage lies in the fact that its sinuous form slows down the evaporation of the metabisulphate solution.

Above all, do not forget to install the little plastic cover on the lock, whichever type you may choose; this will slow evaporation.

The Hydrometer, the Baster, and the Cylinder

One instrument which is used continually throughout the winemaking process is the hydrometer (sometimes known as the densimeter). This is another surprisingly simple instrument of incontestable effectiveness. Usually, the hydrometer is graduated with three scales, the specific gravity (S.G.) scale which is the one most often consulted, the Balling degree, or Brix scale (also used to read specific gravity, particularly in laboratory research in several countries), and finally, the scale used to measure the potential alcohol rate (discussed in greater detail in Chapter 7).

To carry out a density reading with the hydrometer, the home winemaker needs three items: 1) a suction-bulb dropper (this can be a gravy baster) to extract must or wine from the primary or secondary fermentor, 2) a cylinder or testing jar into which the extracted must or wine is poured, and 3) the hydrometer.

The hydrometer itself is a small graduated tube with a weighted bulb at one end which contains a specific constant mass. This hermetically-sealed, air-filled tube can gauge the specific gravity and evaluate the density of the must quite accurately. We recommend using the 30 cm. (12 in.) hydrometer instead of the 15 cm. (6 in.) one.

Place the hydrometer inside its standard testing jar or cylinder. Using the baster, add wine or must for the hydrometer rod to float; a reading can then be taken, at the point where the hydrometer emerges from the must or wine. Because the sugar contained in grape-must is denser than alcohol (the specific gravity of alcohol is 0.792, while that of distilled water is 1.000/0.0 Brix-Balling), the hydrometer readings will always be higher before fermentation than after it, when the sugar has largely been transformed into alcohol. The density, or specific gravity of unfermented grape must is normally

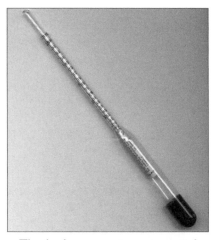

The hydrometer is an essential instrument in winemaking.

between 1.075 and 1.095, depending on the amount of sugar contained in the must. When fermentation has taken place, the S.G. reading will be between 0.990 and 0.995 for dry wines, and between 0.995 and 0.998 for wines that are either sweeter or less alcoholic.

There is a new type of hydrometer cylinder that can be dipped directly into the must or wine to obtain a sample for a specific gravity reading (sold under the brand name of Wine Thief by the Fermtech company). Place the hydrometer inside the cylinder and lower it through the neck of the carboy (or into the primary fermentor) to draw in a sample by means of the pres-

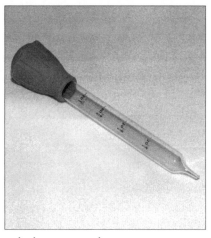

A dropper, or baster, to extract must or wine.

sure valve at its tip. Draw in enough liquid for the hydrometer to float when the cylinder is in a vertical position, then take the

The Wine Thief, a hydrometer cylinder equipped with a valve.

specific gravity reading. The wine or must can be returned to the carboy (or to the primary fermentor) by gently pressing the bottom tip of the cylinder on the neck of the carboy (or on the side of the primary fermentor) which will open the valve and release the contents. Costing a little more than the ordinary cylinder, this device is effective and practical.

The advantage of using a hydrometer is that it makes it easy to verify if the fermentation stage has been successful. After 21 days of fermentation, the hydrometer reading should be less than 1.000. If the reading is higher, it means that the fermentation has stopped before it should have, and that it must be started up again.

The Thermometer

The thermometer measures the temperature of the must. Two types are available.

The first type resembles a hydrometer. It is dipped into the must (don't worry, it floats!) and will register the exact temperature. It is better to use a longer thermometer (30 cm. or 12 in., like the larger model of hydrometer described above): if it falls in, it will be easier to find when it is covered by frothing must in full ferment!

The second type of thermometer is a plastic adhesive strip which is stuck onto the outer surface of the primary fermentor or the carboy. This digital thermometer gives a temperature reading the instant it touches the side of the fermentor. It is inexpensive and very practical, easy to read and instantaneous; moreover, it cannot contaminate the must.

The thermometer is helpful during the alcoholic, or primary fermentation stage, the malolactic fermentation stage, and also during the bulk aging stage.

Carboy Stoppers (or Bungs)

Stoppers for carboys or demi-johns come in several different sizes. Therefore, it is a good idea to purchase the stopper when buying the container, instead of finding out later that it doesn't fit. You will

°F	°C
86	30
84	29
82	28
81	27
79	26
77	25
75	24
73	23
72	22
70	21
68	20
66	19

Digital thermometers are rapidly supplanting glass ones.

know the size is correct when about two-thirds of the stopper enters the neck of the carboy. If the stopper cannot go deep enough, it may eventually move upward, allowing air to get into the carboy. On the other hand, if its diameter is too small, the result may be just as disastrous: the stopper may end up at the bottom of the carboy, which is quite a bother.

Most stoppers for home winemaking are made of rubber, the ideal material because of its elasticity. Rubber can, however, give your wine an unpleasant taste if the stopper is situated too close to the wine's surface. There should be at least five centimetres (2 inches) between the bottom of the stopper and the surface of the wine.

Silicone stoppers have been available for some years now: these do not change the taste of the wine. However, if the proper precautions are not taken, this kind of stopper tends to rise

Silicone bungs.

up suddenly, allowing air to enter the recipient. To prevent this from happening, push the stopper into the neck of the carboy, then press down strongly to make sure it will stay in place. At this point, the fermentation lock can be installed, which gives the stopper, or bung, an additional tightness within the neck. Silicone stoppers stay in place very well if they are inserted in this manner, and will give full satisfaction. They are not fitted for S-shaped fermentation locks, however: the opening to install the lock is a little bit too large for this. Therefore, it is better to use the cylindrical type of fermentation lock with this kind of bung.

The latest rubber bungs available.

Hollow rubber bungs have recently become available. Their outer wall stops up the neck of the carboy effectively, while a hollow cylinder rising from their base can accomodate a fermentation lock. These stoppers are very malleable and can be easily removed from the carboy neck. Also, their concave recess will collect any leakage from the fermentation lock.

Bottling Equipment

Bottles

Bottling is the last crucial stage of home winemaking. You should have enough bottles ready to be able to store and age your wine. Of course, bottles can be bought especially for this purpose, but why not recycle your own, your friends' or your neighbours' bottles? In any case, all bottles must be thoroughly washed with detergent and carefully rinsed. To make this task easier, there are several inexpensive utensils and devices to help you out. These are described below.

The Bottle-Rinser

Although they are not included in basic winemaking kits, bottle-rinsers are extremely useful for cleaning the bottoms of bottles, even of carboys. This little apparatus screws on to the kitchen tap (an adapter may be necessary, depending on the type of spout) and shoots water forcefully right to the bottom of the bottles. It dislodges any dirt or residue very effectively and saves you the trouble of scrubbing with a bottle brush. It is well worth its price (about $20 Cdn.).

A bottle-rinsers is a necessity when recycling bottles.

The Drainer Stand

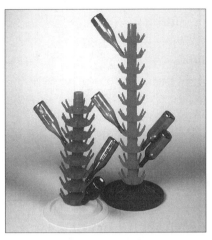

Drainer stands.

The nickname of this piece of equipment is "the Christmas tree." Its trunk is circled by several levels of "branches" pointing upward and slightly outward. These hold the upside-down bottles by their necks so that the water left inside completely drains out into the pan at the base of the drainer. This method prevents water from accumulating inside the bottles, inviting bacterial contamination.

Once the bottles are completely dry (the two models of drainer hold 44 and 88 bottles respectively), they can either be put into cardboard boxes, or simply left on the "tree."

A great time-saver: a sulphiter for disinfecting bottles.

The Sulphiter

This apparatus, which can be installed at the top of the bottle-drainer, is also an extremely practical instrument. It consists of a basin with a fountain jet, or rod, in the middle; standard metabisulphite solution is poured into the basin and the neck of the inverted bottle is fitted over the rod. When the bottle is forced downwards, the pressure makes the jet squirt out a strong rush of solution into the bottle, completely disinfecting the inside of it. This apparatus also costs about $20 Cdn., and is worth its weight in gold for the time it saves. Without it, you would have to pour the meta solution into each bottle with a funnel, swish it around, then funnel it into the next bottle, and so forth. The sulphiter accomplishes the same operation in a single movement, with the solution returning to the basin without any waste. Another advantage of this little machine is that the sulphur fumes are largely prevented from escaping into the surrounding air.

The Bottle-Filler

An essential aid to home winemaking, the bottle-filler is a rigid plastic tube with a siphon valve, or clack valve, on one end. The other end is attached to the flexible tube which will draw the wine from the carboy. The rigid tube is then inserted into the bottle to be filled. By pressing it down against the bottom of the bottle, a rod pushes up to open the valve, allowing the wine to flow into the bottle. When the bottle-filler is lifted out, the flow is cut off as the valve closes. Thus, a bottle can be filled in the twinkling of an eye, with almost no

A stop-start bottle-filler.

mess (careful, the rod gets stuck sometimes!) as long as you pay attention to the mounting level of wine in the bottle. For approximately $4 Cdn., it's practically a gift!

The automatic bottle-filler: easier than the manual one, but more expensive too.

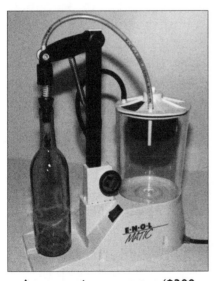

An expensive apparatus ($300 Cdn.), the Enolmatic is for makers of large quantities of wine.

The Automatic Bottle-Filler

A bit more expensive, but even more practical, the automatic bottle filler is placed over the neck of a bottle and fills it to the standard level. It has a secondary tube which takes off the excess wine or foam, and empties it into another recipient beside the bottle. It does the same job as the simple bottle-filler, but also prevents any overflow.

The Enolmatic

The Enolmatic is another, more sophisticated bottle-filler. Its high price ($300 Cdn.) makes it a piece of equipment that is only worthwhile for people who produce relatively large quantities of wine. It is a vacuum pump that works by suction. It can be hooked up to a filtering apparatus, and can also be used for racking. One marked advantage of this machine is that, because it encloses the wine in a vacuum, it decreases the risk of bacterial contamination.

Corkers

If you decide to provide yourself with a corking apparatus, above all, stay away from models which are not free-standing, as they require superhuman effort and patience. The metal corking stand is almost indestructible and very efficient. It only takes a few seconds to cork a bottle and there is hardly ever any mess if you handle the corker and the corks with care. The important thing is

The corker.

to place the bottle in the proper position; the procedure will then be smooth and successful.

Many home winemakers buy corkers because of their incontestable usefulness. The best kind of corking stand is not very expensive (about $50 Cdn.), considering its excellent durability. If you do not want to buy one, they can also be rented from your retailer at fees varying between $2 and $4 per day.

Natural Corks

Several different varieties of corks exist; therefore, you should be sure which type is best suited for your winemaking purposes. For example, if you are intending to make a "28-day" type of wine which will be drunk as soon as it is ready, there is no reason for you to buy corks that last for years. It is best to consult your retailer for expert advice on which type of cork to use.

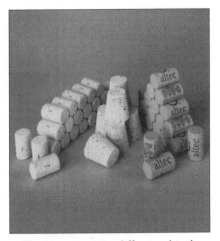

There are many different kinds
of corks.

Bottle with plastic stopper and
Champagne wire, and capsules.

Plastic Stoppers and Champagne Wires

If you wish to make a sparkling wine, you will have to use plastic Champagne stoppers (corks are very difficult to manipulate when making sparkling wines by the traditional method) and tie them down with Champagne wires to keep them from popping out. You will find the necessary material at your winemaking supply store.

Capsules and Labels

Most amateur winemakers love dressing up their full bottles. You can easily procure ready-made plastic and metallic capsules (the latter type is mostly used for sparkling wines) in a variety of shades and colours, to cover the tops of your bottles.

A large variety of labels are also available; they usually come in packages of 30 each, at a price of about $3 Cdn. They identify your production in a decorative way; they have glue on their reverse sides, for wetting and applying to the bottles.

Capsules give wine bottles a
classy, professional appearance.

Labels are held in high esteem
by amateur winemakers.

More Expensive, Specialized Equipment

The Siphon Pump

For those who make a lot of wine, a siphon pump may become a necessity. This is simply an electric pump which siphons wine from one carboy to another. Siphon pumps cost quite a lot (between $200 and $300 Cdn.) and are only worthwhile for domestic winemakers who turn out 500 bottles or more every year, or if the amateur winemaker has back problems, making it risky or painful to lift 20- or 23-litre carboys. This type of pump can also be used to filter wine.

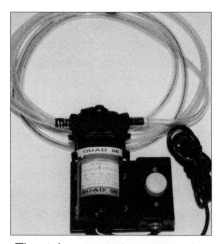

The siphon pump is an expensive
apparatus which may be
necessary for winemakers
with back problems.

The Wine Filter

More and more home winemakers filter their wine for the simple reason that they are proud of it, and want it to compare

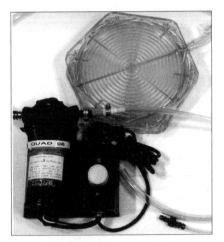

favourably in appearance with the wines available in stores. And in fact, filtered home-made wines often do attain the clearness of most commercial wines.

Many retailers will lend filtering equipment to their regular customers (or rent them at a very modest fee), but some home winemakers prefer to own their own apparatus. This way, they save themselves the trouble of putting their names on a

One model of wine filter.

lengthy waiting list at the winemaking store when the season is at its height.

There are two kinds of wine filters, pressure and vacuum pump filters. Recently, a device which can be fitted with filter cartridges has become available: it is quite effective but not yet perfect. Your best bet is still filtering equipment that incorporates a compressor or a pump.

Filters have different grades of porosity; the wine can be passed through a first set of coarse filters, then through a second set of finer filters, thus attaining perfect clarity.

One little inconvenience arises in filtering: the hydrochloric acid that is used in manufacturing the filter pads must be washed out. This is a rather lengthy operation. We can only hope that soon we will no longer be obliged to circulate water (about 5 gallons of it), then metabisulphite solution ($1/4$ gallon), and finally, distilled water (another gallon) through the pads before using them for the wine!

Filtering apparatus need not be very expensive. Some machines sell at only $50 Cdn., although it may cost you up to $400 if a compressor or a pump is included. We recommend that you buy the most expensive and the best-quality filtering apparatus available. Otherwise, it is better to continue borrowing or renting from your wine equipment store.

If you intend to buy a wine filter, investigate all the products available to be able to choose the best. We will soon be publishing a guide to wine filters: you might want to read it before deciding. Waiting might also be a good policy because in this area, new and better products are continually being developed.

The Grape Crusher

Winemakers who use whole grapes as the raw material for their wine, instead of must in one of its forms, need to borrow, rent, or buy two essential (and costly) instruments, the crusher and the press. The crusher is a kind of grinder in the form of a large funnel with a toothed roller at the bottom which is turned by a handle to break open the grapes (without crushing the seeds), allowing the pulp to release its juice.

A grape crusher.

More sophisticated electric crushers exist, which, as you might expect, cost much more than the manual model. A destemming mechanism is built into some of these.

The Wine Press

The grapes that have gone through the crusher are then pressed to obtain all of their juice. The wine press is a barrel made of unjoined wooden lathes with an apparatus at the top to press the grapes. It is activated by tightening the vise around the large central screw which forces a round lid down onto the grapes, squeezing their juice out at the bottom and through the spaces between the lathes. The operation continues until the grapes have released all their juice.

In this area too, some models are more efficient (and more expensive) than others.

A wine press.

This concludes our section on the basic equipment used in home wine production. The list is fairly complete. It will give the prospective home winemaker a good idea of the utensils and instruments that he or she needs for the entire process. Of course, we could add others, for example, funnels (very useful at times), and larger siphons for water flow inside the carboys, etc., but the items that we have listed above will certainly stand you in good stead until you develop your own personal style of winemaking, perhaps leading to further requirements.

CHAPTER 5

The Choice of Must

In the previous chapter, we presented an inventory of the equipment necessary to make wine at home. Once these items have been obtained, it is time to buy the must[1] best suited to your purposes. Some amateurs like to drink their wine as soon as possible, while others prefer to wait a year before opening their first bottle.

Whichever course you decide upon, we strongly recommend that you seek advice from an experienced retailer of must. He or she will be able to tell you which must is appropriate for making a wine that matures early, or a wine that will be much better after a certain amount of aging. The essential thing is that you be aware of all the possibilities open to you, as there are several different ways that you can make your wine.

In this chapter, we will present an overview of the musts available. We will pay particular attention to the methods of concentrating the juice, and with good reason: if home winemaking has grown by leaps and bounds over the last fifty years, it is due to the technique of concentration, which allows a wide variety of musts to travel across the world without spoiling or fermenting.

---

1. A reminder that the term "must" refers to grape juice destined for fermentation. It may contain skins and stems or not.

Concentrated Musts

Concentrated musts were the first to become generally available to home winemakers, who were previously limited to buying whole fresh wine grapes at the market in October. The high demand has incited the producers of concentrated musts to develop an increasingly sophisticated technology to improve their product and to occupy a bigger share of the market.

A refrigerated tanker truck carrying fresh must.

However, the marketing of sterilized and refrigerated fresh musts has turned this situation around, with the producers of fresh must gaining on producers of concentrates as far as demand is concerned. One thing is certain: with the possiblility of transporting must in refrigerated tanker trucks, fresh and sterilized musts have become increasingly popular over the past ten years.

Concentration Techniques

The technique of concentrating must has been practised for more than 100 years. This process allows the must to be preserved for a period long beyond the grape harvest season. The preserved musts can be transported to other localities or other countries, where they are diluted with purified water and fermented to become wine.

Over the last thirty years, there has been considerable progress in developing more sophisticated techniques to preserve the inherent character of the grapes. This technology has progressed from boiling directly over a fire or a heating element to a very complex process that works by osmosis.

Concentration by Boiling

The earliest method used to concentrate grape must simply consisted in boiling the must until a large part of the water contained in it had evaporated.

The concentrated must obtained by this method could be more easily transported than in its more voluminous original state. Concentrate was also easier to transport because the pasteurization that occurred during boiling prevented any possibility of unwanted fermentation. The concentrated must could therefore be kept until the winemaker decided to start the fermentation process.

The practice of this simple and natural concentration technique produced certain side-effects intrinsic to the method, that is, the high temperature required to boil the must resulted in "burn" (or caramelization). The wines made from this type of must could unfortunately be distinguished from traditionally-produced wines by their "burnt" taste, eventually discouraging a good number of amateur winemakers who were disappointed by the results.

Concentration under Vacuum

To minimize the caramelization effect, engineers invented a way to boil the must under a partial vacuum. This allows evaporation to occur at lower temperatures, thus considerably decreasing the burn phenomenon. Also, the juice is sprayed onto the heated walls of the boiler to make the evaporation occur more rapidly than it does in ordinary boiling. The steam is evacuated by vacuum pressure, leaving only the concentrate. By obtaining the appropriate relationship between the vacuum pressure and the temperature of the must, it is possible to produce a concentrate (the volume being reduced from 4.5 litres to 1 litre!) with a much less discernible caramel taste. This technique is clearly superior to simple boiling. However, these products should not be purchased with blind confidence, as certain types of vacuum apparatus are more effective than others. In fact, vacuum-evaporation techniques have considerably evolved since they were first tried; therefore, a concentrated must made with more recently-developed technology will probably be a better bet than concentrates made with older systems.

Concentration by Cryogenization

Concentration by cryogenization has been practised for several years now and has produced excellent results. In this technique, the temperature of the must is lowered, turning the water in the must into ice which can then be removed, leaving only the concentrated must. The idea of proceeding in reverse, by freezing instead of heating the must, was a stroke of genius. The caramelization factor is completely eliminated and as a bonus, the full bouquet of the wine is protected! The fly in the ointment: the high cost of this process is transferred to the retail price of the must. Therefore, not many of these musts are sold on the market, precisely because of their prohibitive production costs.

Concentration by Osmosis

Another method which has proved successful in conserving the natural flavours of the must is concentration by osmosis. This technique simply relies on pressure. The must is blocked by a low-porosity filter which allows only the water to pass through it. This same technique of concentration by osmosis, which is by no means new, is used in concentrating the raw maple sap collected to make maple syrup. In the case of wine, the higher acid content has made it necessary to carry out major and extremely complex technological modifications to this basic technique.

The results have been quite impressive, although in this concentration method as well as in the preceding one, the high costs of the procedure (with the resulting undesirable trickle-down effect on retail prices) have caused winemakers to adopt a wait-and-see strategy, in hopes that the prices will go down. At the moment, only one company, in Australia, produces musts concentrated by osmosis, offering a nice selection of Chardonnay, Cabernet Sauvignon, and Riesling musts. However, until now, Japanese clientele has been buying up almost all of the company's stock as soon as it is available!

This is unfortunate, because when it is concentrated by osmosis, the must loses almost none of its inherent character, even if a few precautions must be taken to maintain its balance, and to protect it against the proliferation of bacteria. This concentration technique appears to be the most promising one, as long as production costs can be brought down within reasonable limits. Up to now, only a few retailers have been able to obtain musts concentrated by osmosis.

The Availability of Concentrated Musts

There are presently a large variety of concentrated musts on the market. Most of these, as explained above, have been concentrated by one of the evaporation methods, and techniques vary considerably from one company to another. How can you find your way in all of this? It is best to rely on the advice of your winemaking retailer, and also, on the infallible method of trial and error.

In any case, you should read all you can about the different types of must available, to have a better idea of the value of the respective products before making your choice.

Concentrates in the 3-Litre (100 oz.) Format

For a long time, the 3-litre format has been considered the standard volume for concentrated must, and it has certainly been the most popular one for many years. It contains 3 litres (100 oz.) of concentrate at a rate of 4 $^1/_2$ to 1. The concentrated must is usually packaged directly by the producer at its place of origin. At the standard concentration rate, three litres will allow you to make between 19 and 23 litres of wine [2]. If you do not add as much water as directed, your wine will have too much body and tannin, but if you stretch it beyond 23 litres [3] the wine will be thin and insipid.

It is important to know that this kind of concentrate (sold in a metal container, or in a plastic bag inside a box) is not balanced in acids and sugar, and therefore, you will have to carry out those operations yourself. You will also have to procure the necessary packets of additives (clarifiers, stabilizer, etc.), as well as approximately 2 kilos (4.4 lbs.) of sugar to be able to produce a wine with an alcohol content of about 12%. Full instructions are usually provided with the concentrate.

The first time that concentrated must was sold to the public, it was in this format. Even if a bit more work is required and the margin of error is greater, wines produced from this product continue to amaze us. Experienced winemakers can use it with full confidence and experiment with their own blends.

---

2. You may notice that the amount of water to be added is greater than the quantity that was removed from the must in the concentration process. It was found that if the must was reconstituted with the same proportion of water, the wine produced had too much body and was overly tannic.

3. For the equivalents in Imperial and U.S. measures, see page 189.

The 3-Litre Format Kit

The home winemaker can also procure a 3-litre format kit, containing all the elements needed to produce the wine. This type of kit generally includes the following:

a) the concentrated must;

b) a packet containing the acids and tannin to balance the must;

c) yeast;

d) one or two clarifying agents;

e) a stabilizing agent.

Thus, the winemaker does not have to worry about the acidity (the pH level), because the balancing has already been worked out. Besides the basic equipment shown in the preceding chapter of this book, the only thing needed is to add the purified water and sugar to the must in the proportions indicated in the directions.

Buying a kit makes the winemaking process even easier, and especially because the balancing process is taken care of, the demand for this product has overtaken the demand for concentrate sold by itself.

Here too, the results have often been quite astonishing, giving full satisfaction to winemakers who have become enthusiastic converts.

The 5 or 5.5-Litre (200 - 250 oz.) Format Kit

This is the most popular kit format available; the degree of concentration is weaker than in the preceding formats. Already balanced in sugar and tannins, this concentrate comes in a plastic bag (inside a cardboard box). The customary additives (yeast, clarifiers and stabilizers) are included, with directions for use. In both the 5-litre and the 5.5-litre format, the concentrate will produce 23 litres of wine. It is available in a wide range of grape varieties (eg. Cabernet Sauvignon and

Chenin Blanc) and wine types (eg. Burgundy, Chianti, Valpoli-
cella, etc.).

Making wine with these kits is a relatively simple operation, as you just have to add purified water and follow the steps
that are very clearly explained
in the directions. The quality
of each type of concentrate is
reflected in its retail price,
which varies considerably
from one brand to the next,
and from one grape variety or
blend to another. Some concentrates have been kept at
low temperatures and must be
made into wine as soon as
they are taken out of refrigeration, whereas others may stay
at room temperature for
months without any problem.

The results can be
remarkable: the quality of the

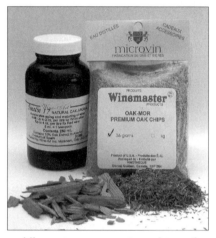

All musts can acquire a hint of
oak aging with the addition of
oak chips or essence.

wines made from these products—especially if care is taken in
the production process, and if they are allowed to age ade-
quately—often surpasses that of the non-*appellation* wines
available on the market.

In building up a supply of wine, the amateur winemaker
will obtain good results from this product: wines that are easily prepared, reliable, and well-liked. Many types of wine prepared in this manner can be drunk almost right after bottling,
but all of them will improve by aging for a few months, and can
be kept for about three years, depending of course on factors
such as how the wine is bottled, the type of cork used, and the
temperature that the wine is stored at.

Semi-Concentrated Musts

The term "semi-concentrate" refers to concentrated must to which pasteurized (sterilized) must has been added. Semi-concentrates come in plastic bags (inside attractive cardboard boxes or plastic pails); they are recent arrivals on the market, and have been selling very successfully.

The recipe is simple: pure sterilized must is added to the concentrate to heighten the bouquet of the wine that will be made from it. The quantity added varies among the different producers, and is usually a closely-guarded secret. The proportion of sterilized must present determines whether just a small amount, or no sugar at all will be added when making the wine from the concentrate. Semi-concentrates are available in 8-litre and 15-litre formats with additives included. The winemaker only has to add 8 or 15 litres of purified water to produce 23 litres of wine, depending on the degree of concentration.

Packaging differs among producers as well. Mosti Mondiale, a pioneer in this area, began selling this format in a triangular carton, then adopted a plastic pail.

It is very easy to make wine from semi-concentrates: along with the simple addition of water, the directions are not at all complicated, and good wine can be made with a minimum of time and effort.

The wines made from the 15-litre format are more complex than those produced from the 8-litre format; several can be drunk right after bottling, and all of them age well. Due to the addition of the unadulterated grape must, some of these wines develop an extraordinary flavour and bouquet after aging for a year or so. They will keep well from two to four years if aged in an appropriate cellar.

In this category as well, quality and price closely correspond: the more you pay, the greater the probability that you will be buying a better-quality product. For the best choice according to your needs, we again advise you to consult your winemaking specialist. It cannot be denied: generally speaking, semi-concentrates are superior to plain concentrates in flavour and in quality, depending, of course, on the standards and conscientiousness of the companies that produce them.

Sterilized Musts

Even newer on the market, developed by the Mosti Mondiale company, pure sterilized musts are bound for glory. Also referred to as pasteurized musts, they are sold in a 23-litre format and are more expensive than concentrates and semi-concentrates. However, they generally make better-quality wine.

The advantage of sterilized must is that it is always available. Moreover, it is completely whole and natural. Nothing has been added to it; it has simply been sterilized and balanced with products that are found naturally in wine, such as tartaric acid and tannin. It is also colour-enhanced naturally with pigment obtained from tinting grapes.

Winemakers who appreciate sterilized must are usually willing to spend a bit more for a product which is not only better quality, but which does not have to undergo the malolactic fermentation stage as fresh grapes and fresh musts do. Thus, the amateur of sterilized must aims for superior quality "within a reasonable delay," as the wines made from it can be drunk younger than wine made from whole grapes or from unsterilized fresh must.

The results are very satisfactory, sometimes even spectacular!

Fresh Musts

Available in 20- and 23-litre formats, fresh refrigerated musts are radically changing the home winemaking scene. They first appeared on the market about ten years ago. They are 100% fresh musts that have already been balanced and inoculated with selected yeast. Therefore, they are ready for fermentation without further ado.

Refrigerated just near their freezing point, these musts start to ferment as soon as they lose their chill. Of all the types of must available, this one is the closest to whole grapes, but without the inconvenience and expense of crushing and pressing, as all the grape residue has been removed.

Fresh musts can produce spectacular results.

Fresh refrigerated musts are not sterilized, so they may eventually undergo malolactic fermentation. This fermentation stage must be properly dealt with if you do not want the corks to shoot out of their bottles during the aging process! (Explanations of the malolactic fermentation stage are found in Chapters 2 and 6 of this book.)

Fresh musts are available mainly in the autumn when the wine grapes are harvested, but they can be found throughout the year if producers feel that there is a sufficient demand for them. Musts from some grape varieties sell out very quickly, while others remain available much longer.

Although making wine from fresh must requires a little more care, the results can be of quite exceptional quality (although some years are better than others, of course). Many winemakers swear by this form of must, as they have found it most rewarding.

Another appreciable advantage of fresh musts: because they have not gone through the pasteurization process, they generally cost a bit less than the sterilized musts.

Musts From Whole Grapes

Home winemaking beginning from whole grapes is still very popular, particularly among North Americans of Italian, Spanish, Portuguese, or Greek origin, many of whom have fairly elaborate production systems at home. Unfortunately, the resulting wine is often harsh or semi-sparkling, mainly because archaic techniques are used. Winemaking according to the time-honoured traditional method requires considerable know-how and equipment, as well as good, mature grapes. An amateur winemaker who cannot distinguish among the many varieties of grapes available is in danger of being greatly disappointed when the first bottle is opened. We will not beat around the bush: wait until you have quite a lot of skill and experience behind you before trying to make wine this way. Even old hands occasionally suffer bitter reversals in this delicate art.

None the less, Chapter 6 of this book does offer instruction and advice in the art of winemaking with whole grapes.

Pure Musts vs. Blends

The quality of a must mainly depends on the grapes that go into it. We can easily imagine that the makers of concentrated, sterilized, or fresh musts do their utmost to provide the best possible product in order to satisfy an increasingly discriminating clientele.

Naturally, these producers would like nothing better than to offer their customer musts made from the most prestigious Burgundy or Bordeaux grapes, at competitive prices. Unfortunately, not only these classic varieties, but French wine grapes in general are the most difficult to obtain. In France, national laws established to protect the wine industry set quotas for vintners: grapes that surpass the quota must go to growers' cooperatives where they are mixed with other varieties. Thus, buyers of grapes for must never have access to the top-name French varieties, but are only able to buy "generic" regional varieties, which are in fact a blend of several grape varieties. This is why you will never see the names of the great French vineyards on commercial must containers.

Laws are less strict in other wine-producing countries, allowing dealers of must to buy their raw material from among the classic grape varieties. Producers have seized the occasion, and therefore more good-quality single-variety musts are becoming available to home winemakers.

This choice exists, but it is far from being the norm. The majority of the must-seller's stock consists of generic grapes bought wholesale on the different world markets. The producer has to do what he or she can with them to produce the best quality of must possible in the circumstances. To offset the homogenizing effect of a mixture of grape varieties and to create a distinctive type of must, some oenological experts add the extract of certain fruits (peach, pear, and raspberry, for example), or resort to what practically amounts to a breach of ethics in wine production: the addition of artificial flavouring.

The Art of Blending

The expert faced with the task of blending different types of concentrated must strives to achieve a blend which will give predictable and consistent results. A must can be said to produce a wine resembling a Burgundy or an Alsace wine, for example. The term "type" often occurs in the names of commercialized must: "Burgundy type" or "Bordeaux type" clearly specifies that the wine made from that must should taste like a wine from that particular region, or even like a particular varietal from that region. The fact is, however, the must is probably not made from that variety of grapes at all, but from grapes from different parts of the world which have been blended to make the resulting wine taste as if it has been made from that variety.

There are musts available which are identified by the name of a single variety, for example, "Cabernet Sauvignon," "Chardonnay," or "Riesling". This means that the must in question is constituted wholly or partially of the grape variety marked on the container. The problem is that there are no laws, either in Canada or in the United States, requiring that the must be constituted wholly of the grape variety marked on the label. Thus, a producer can perfectly well label a must a Cabernet Sauvignon, when the must in question only contains 40 % of that variety!

A Voluntary Ethical Standard

In the area of naming commercial brands of must, there exists a lamentable no-man's-land in the legislation which governmental authorities are not in hurry to fill up. Apparently, they prefer to leave amateur winemakers in doubt so as not to overly encourage artisanal production and self-sufficiency in this area! In spite of this loophole in labelling regulations, the majority of must-producers hold to a voluntary ethical standard, ensuring that at least half of the contents corresponds to the variety indicated on the label. This is better than nothing, but it is still not good enough. The company selling the must should at least clearly mark the percentage of the advertised variety with respect to the other grape types blended into it. In any case, we are well aware that it is almost impossible to find a must containing 100 % of a classic variety for sale in a winemaking store. This is logical, given the fact that even the *appellation contrôlée* wines as well as the *vins délimités de qualité supérieure* (the second rank of *appellations* in France) contain a proportion of assemblage wines which reaches 25 % in many cases. Aren't the *grands crus* elaborated with a certain proportion of less noble varietals? For example, the greatest Bordeaux red, first-growth Château Lafite Rothschild, is composed of 70 % Cabernet Sauvignon, 5 % Cabernet Franc, 20 % Merlot, and 5 % Petite Verdot grapes. As for Châteauneuf du Pape, it is made from up to 13 varietals! Assemblage [4] is such an accepted practice that even the State of California, while upholding puritanical standards in many other aspects of the wine industry, has surrendered to it. The great California wines (Mondavi, Joe Heitz, Beaulieu, Ridge Vineyards) are now allowed to be assembled as long as they contain a minimum 75 % of the variety indicated on the label.

In truth, the blending of musts is a felicitous practice which can correct inherent defects in the mainstay variety (deficient tannin, too much astringency, a too-pale colour, etc.) and is of benefit to all concerned when it is carried out with inspired intuition, intelligence and precise care.

Paying for Good Value

The quality of home-made wine is directly related to the value of its ingredients. Thus, to be able to sell kits at low prices, the quality of the concentrate is sacrificed, or part of the concentrate is replaced by colouring and sugar. In this domain, as in most others, there are no miracles, just as there is no substitute for good quality. This is why we advise our readers to always choose the best. It will cost you an average of 25 or 50 cents more per bottle, but you will be infinitely more satisfied. In any case, you need to be careful. To give an example, some companies sell sterilized musts that have been adulterated, partially or totally. That is, these musts are not 100 % pure, but are composed of reconstituted concentrated must. Therefore, you should always read the labels attentively and consult your retailer to know about the processing methods involved. It would be ludicrous to pay a higher price for what

---

4. The term "assemblage wines" applies to wines made from different varieties grown in the same vineyard, whereas blending is the result of mixing grapes grown in different vineyards, regions, countries, or even continents.

is simply a concentrate to which the producer has added water; you can do the same operation yourself and pay less!

An additional quality criteria for concentrated must should be its age. Heavy in sugar and acidity, concentrates have a limited conservation time, depending on storage temperatures. You shouldn't be surprised to discover that there is a marked difference in flavour between a wine made from fresh concentrate and one made from concentrate which has been allowed to sit on the shelf too long. Here too, it would be a significant improvement if producers of must were obliged to indicate a "best before," or expiry date on their product, a practice which is almost ubiquitous in the food industry today.

An Enlightened Choice

To be able to choose the appropriate kind of must for your needs, it is best to become familiar with winemakers' supply shops, which are fortunately becoming more common in most cities and towns. There, amateurs will obtain top information about the different brands and types of musts, as well as good practical advice about most other aspects of home winemaking. The customer can ask questions and take notes on what the retailer has to say about each product. We recommend that you avoid large supermarkets, department stores, and discount megastores when buying must, as you may only obtain incomplete and vague information from salespeople who are not experts in this domain.

Of course, every winemaker has his or her own individual criteria. Those who want to make table wines that can be drunk as young as possible will have a choice among several brands and types of concentrated must which will give them satisfaction.

On the other hand, more patient amateurs who prefer to take the additional time necessary to obtain a richer and more complex wine are advised to look into semi-concentrated, sterilized, or fresh musts. They will have to pay more and wait longer, but it will be worth the trouble.

The Lifespan of Home-Made Wine

Home-made wine, just like the table wines sold in stores, does not last anything near the length of time that the finest wines do.

This is understandable: the home wine market consists mainly of people who want to drink their wine within a reasonably short time (with many among them finding it impossible to wait until their production reaches full maturity before trying a bottle!).

These home winemakers do not want to increase the amount of tannin in their must; on the contrary, they would rather try to attenuate its effects in a wine intended for drinking very young. The consequence of this approach is that home-made wines meant for drinking young cannot age as long as fine wines, which have a much higher tannin content than wines destined for everyday consumption. In fact, in the case of most of the *grand crus*, it is not advisable to drink them until 5 or 10 years after bottling.

The Wine Maturation Graph

To give winemakers a more precise idea of the maturation times of wines made from the different types of must (concentrated, semi-concentrated, sterilized, or fresh), we have included a Wine Maturation Graph (on page 117). You will notice that wine made from concentrates have a shorter lifespan than wine made from whole must. This is due to two factors. The first factor concerns the wine's body: wines made from concentrate, precisely because they have been reconstituted, have a less complex particle balance and a lower proportion of solid matter than wines made from pure must. The other factor relates to the alcohol content: most of the wines made from concentrates are meant for drinking young (like the "28-day" concentrate kits); because of this, they contain less alcohol, a component which contributes positively in the aging of wine. For these reasons, wines made from concentrated musts have a shorter drinking life (from 10 months to three years after fermentation) than those made from sterilized musts (one to four years). As for wines made from fresh must, their lifespan is even longer, from one to five years, on the average.

In the Wine Maturation Graph on the following page, a horizontal line cuts through the curves showing the respective life spans of wines made from the different types of must. This line is referred to as the Tasting Limit: its first intersection with the curves indicates the minimum maturing time before opening the first bottle of wine made from each particular type of must. The second intersection (with the same curves) represents the maximum time that the wine made from that type of must can be safely stored without losing its flavour or even becoming undrinkable.

As seen in the Graph, home-made wine can be drunk as early as two months after fermentation (although it is always better to wait for three months). This minimal standard applies to all wines, except those made from fresh must, which can only be drunk after six months of maturation. This said, all home-made wines taste better after one year of aging. It is at the one-year mark (as shown in the Graph) that they reach their full degree of maturity. In the case of wine made from fresh and sterilized must, this plateau lasts longer, and the optimum tasting period can be delayed, as these wines continue to improve for two years and even longer.

It should be noted that wines made from fresh must have a longer life than those made from the other forms of must, often going beyond five years. Some very full-bodied wines made from fresh must (Montepulciano, for example) can be left to age for ten years.

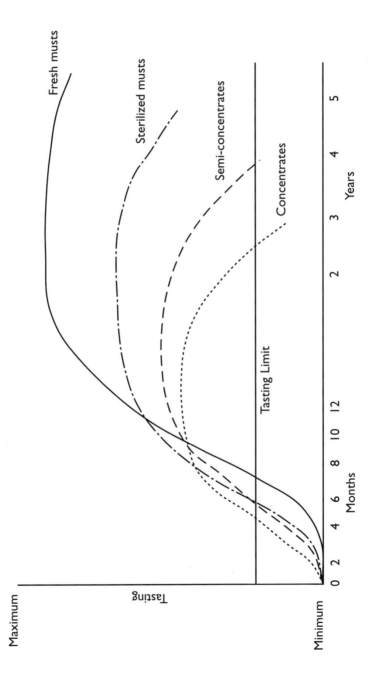

Wine Maturation Graph

Another important factor to consider is that the Graph is based on wine stored at the ideal temperature (between 10°C and 15°C, or 50°F - 59°F) and at a normal humidity rate. It supposes as well that the bottling has been carried out after proper sulphiting and that corks of the appropriate type have been used. If your wine is kept in an apartment at room temperature, its lifespan will be somewhat shorter, as warmer temperatures accelerate the wine's maturation as well as its subsequent decline.

CHAPTER 6

The Winemaking Process

T he winemaking process consists of transforming the grapes into wine. The juice destined for making wine is called the must. The must cannot be transformed into wine without the presence of yeast.

Anyone can make wine from must as long as he or she has the essential equipment, the necessary ingredients and space, observes the important standards of hygiene, and faithfully follows the appropriate directions to obtain the desired results. The operation is simple and success relatively easy if a minimum of care is taken, with attention to certain crucial details. At the risk of being overly repetitive, we remind you that the utensils, instruments and containers used in making the wine must be absolutely clean if you want to avoid disaster. Tubs or pails, carboys and wine bottles, tubing, spoons and stoppers, and even the fermentation lock and the hydrometer must be thoroughly washed, disinfected, and rinsed, to prevent at all costs the proliferation of bacteria that can impair the wine.

We also strongly recommend that you use a winemaking record card, or log. If you don't know how to prepare one yourself, your retailer will probably have them in stock. Filling out this procedural record is an effective precautionary measure when making your own wine, allowing you to refer back to essential data throughout the process. It is not only important to know the initial density (S.G. rate) of the must, but also to

Type: _____ Lot number:_____ Date of purchase:_____

☐ Concentrate   ☐ Semi-concentrate   ☐ Sterile juice   ☐ Fresh must

☐ Other: _____

Base quantity: _____ Litres   Water: _____ Litres   Yield: _____ Litres

FERMENTATION (additions & progression):

Sugar: _____ Yeast nutrient: _____ Bentonite: _____

Acid blend: _____ Tannin/Oak: _____ Other(s): _____

Yeast: _____ Date added to must: _____

Starting S.G.: _____ Temperature of must: _____

Date: _____ S.G.: _____ T° _____ Comments: _____

( ) _____ _____ _____ _____
( ) _____ _____ _____ _____
( ) _____ _____ _____ _____
( ) _____ _____ _____ _____
( ) _____ _____ _____ _____
( ) _____ _____ _____ _____

(R): RACKING

Resting time (in carboy): From: _____ To: _____

FINISHING: (date/quant.)

Final oaking:_____ Stabilizer: _____ Clarifier:_____

Sweetener: _____ Other: _____

FILTERING: Date: _____ Pad #: _____

BOTTLING: Date: _____ Cork #: _____ # of bottles: _____

FERMENTATION CHART:

Masti Mondiale inc.

NOTES, APPRECIATION & COMMENTS AT BACK

A personal winemaking record card.

know exactly when the must was put into the secondary fermentor (carboy), the times and dates that clarifiers or stablizers were added, etc. Comments on occasional tastings can also be noted. These cards will constitute a valuable record of your own development as a competent winemaker. At a later time, you can peruse these accounts of your earlier experiences with the full advantage of hindsight, and probably with an ironical chuckle or two.

The Fermentation Stage: A Very Complex Phenomenon

Home winemaking has become relatively easy in the modern era, principally due to our ability to control the fermentation process. Nonetheless, this process is still an immensely

The primary fermentation stage.

complicated chemical transformation. To describe it in detail would require an advanced knowledge of biochemistry; fully scientific treatises on vinificiation and fermentation are restricted to a relatively small readership and will not concern us here.

It is important to realize, however, that the fermentation process never takes place in exactly the same way from one time to the next. In this sense, the winemaker differs from an artisan who masters the totality of the working procedures and materials at hand, ensuring a certain predictable precision in the final result (a glass-blower, for example, already knows exactly when to blow the glass, and the exact way to shape it). The winemaker is always obliged to let nature participate in determining the composition of the final form of the grape. Sun, rain, cold, heat, the type of soil, the presence of parasites, the grape variety (its age and history, where the wine was grown, the way it was grafted or pruned, etc.): the winemaker can never completely control all of these elements, and therefore, can never predict with absolute certainty exactly how the wine will turn out when the must has fermented. The margin of error is always present to a greater or lesser degree. This is even more evident now that gas chromatography has detected more than 250 components in wine; changes in any of these components (in their quantity, quality, or proportions) will have a relatively noticeable effect on the wine's composition and taste.

And that is not all: although scientific research has given us more effective and predictable yeasts, the winemaker must accept the inherent changeability of their activity and hope that the fermentation process will take place in the desired way. To put it bluntly, the winemaker can go to any lengths to obtain the best possible results, but there is no guarantee in the fermentation process.

Of course, a Château Petrus will always be a Château Petrus, but one vintage to the next will vary in its composition, its aroma, its richness and its depth, and in consequence, there are surprisingly abrupt rises and falls in its selling price through the years. There are good and bad vintage years, no matter how much time, work, and money have been invested to ensure that the Château in question be the best ever. The reason for these fluctuations simply lies in the fact that the grape is a living organism, and as such, does not mature with perfect symmetry. It continually delights and disappoints, with an indifference that tries the patience of those who dedicate their every conscious moment to lovingly taking care of it. In the famous refrain of a certain aria, "love is a gypsy child who has never obeyed any law;" in truth, the wine grape is as provokingly fickle as Bizet's tempestuous heroine.

Preparing Yeast Starter

To induce the fermentation of the must, it is necessary to inoculate it with yeast (this is referred to as "pitching the yeast"). This can simply be done with a packet of yeast, but when there are several fermentors to be started, you can prepare a large quantity of yeast yourself. This starter culture is known in winemaking jargon as *pied de cuve*, and should be carefully watched over, as any error can cause delay and worry.

The preparation of yeast starter is particularly useful for amateurs who carry out their winemaking activities in autumn, when wine grapes and fresh musts arrive from California, Italy, Spain, and other countries where wine grapes are grown.

- To prepare yeast starter, you will need 1 $^1/_4$ litre (40 oz.) of must at room temperature. Whether the must has been reconstituted from concentrate, or whether it is fresh or sterilized must, it is recommended to add some purified water to it [1] to decrease its density slightly. The initial specific gravity (S.G.) reading from the hydrometer should be between 1.060 and 1.070. (Throughout the winemaking process, always remember to sterilize the hydrometer and the utensils by spraying with standard metabilsulphite solution and rinse them with purified water before *every* use.) To avoid any bacterial contamination, we suggest heating the must to 70°C (158°F) for 20 minutes.
- Once the correct density has been attained, proceed according to the directions on the packet of yeast, that is, dissolve the yeast in 60 ml. ($^1/_4$ cup.) of luke-warm water (about 40°C or 104°F) and let it stand at room temperature for 15 minutes. Pour it into another

---

1. By purified water, we mean distilled water or spring water. Tap water, boiled and cooled, is also acceptable.

sterilized container big enough to hold the starter which can be sealed with a fermentation lock and bung.

- Add 125 ml. ($^1/_2$ cup) of the prepared must and close the container with the fermentation lock and bung. Ideally, the yeast starter should be kept at a temperature of 23°C (73°F). If this temperature cannot be maintained, then the next best is normal room temperature (20°C - 22°C, or 68°F - 72°F), and in this case, the waiting time should be half an hour longer than the time indicated below (for the ideal temperature).
- After a waiting time of 1 - 2 hours, depending on the activity of the yeast (if there is strong activity, it will be noticeable in the movement inside the fermentation lock). Do not wait longer than two hours, however, as the yeast may die without further nutrients.
- Now add 250 ml. (8 oz.) of the must to the preparation.
- Replace the fermentation lock and leave the mixture for another hour or two. If the yeast action is sluggish, add one level quarter-teaspoon of yeast nutrients, or yeast energizer (obtainable at a winemakers' supply store).
- After these steps, add a further 500 ml. (2 cups) of must. Proceed in the same way as in the preceding operations, with the same waiting time.
- Finally, add the rest of the must and wait for two hours.

The yeast starter obtained in this way is extremely active and is enough to ferment 200 litres (44 Imp.gal./53 U.S. gal.) of must, that is, 10 standard (20- or 23-litre) fermentors of must, with 125 ml. ($^1/_2$ cup) of yeast starter for each of them.

Preparing yeast starter is not only advantageous from a financial point of view (only one packet of yeast is needed for 10 fermentors), but it is also more effective, as yeast starter induces a much more rapid fermentation than the usual method does.

Restarter

As will be seen further on in this chapter, it sometimes happens that fermentation will stop in the midst of the process. There are several possible reasons for this (see the end of the section on yeast in Chapter 2). Often, stuck fermentation is due to the fact that the winemaker delayed too long in putting the must into the fermentor, or put the fermentor in a

Making restarter.

too-cold place. If fermentation stops and if the specific gravity remains below 1.015, it is highly doubtful that you will be able to restart fermentation by using more packets of yeast. The alcohol content of the must is too high at this point for the cultured yeast to proliferate spontaneously.

The first thing to do in this case is to warm up the must and produce restarter that is acclimatized to a high alcohol rate. Note that if bentonite has been dissolved in the must, racking has to be carried out to get rid of the bentonite before proceeding further; if bentonite is present, it will push the yeast cells down to the bottom of the vat or carboy, and their effectiveness will be greatly diminished.

- The preparation method for restarter is similar to that described in the previous section. However in this case, half a litre (2 cups) is enough to restart the fermentation of 23 litres of must in a vat or carboy. Procure some must (it is a good idea to keep a reserve of must for use in similar circumstances); whether the must is fresh, sterilized, or reconstituted concentrate, some purified water should be added to lower its density. Its specific gravity should be between 1.060 and 1.070 (remember to sanitize the hydrometer before use). To avoid bacterial contamination, it is recommended to keep the must at a temperature of 70°C (158°F) for 20 minutes.

- When the correct density and temperature are attained, the yeast is inoculated. To produce restarter, the yeast should be of a kind that resists a high degree of alcohol: Champagne yeast (*Saccharomyces bayanus*) of the EC-1118 type is the most appropriate yeast for this purpose, as it is cultured specifically to resist a high alcohol strength.

- Following this, the procedure is the same as for yeast starter. Proceed according to the directions on the packet of yeast, that is, dissolve the yeast in 60 ml. (¼ cup) of luke-warm water (about 40°C or 104°F) and let it stand at room temperature for 15 minutes. Pour it into another sterilized container which can be sealed with a fermentation lock and bung.

- Add 125 ml. (½ cup) of the prepared must and close the container with the stopper. The restarter should be kept if possible at 23°C (73°F); if this temperature cannot be maintained, then keep it at room temperature (20°C - 22°C, or 68°F - 72°F) for half an hour longer than the time indicated below.

- After a waiting time of between one and two hours, depending on the activity of the yeast (strong activity will be visible inside the fermentation lock). Do not wait any longer, however, as the yeast will die without more food.

- Add 125 ml. (½ cup) of the must to the preparation.

- Replace the fermentation lock and wait for another hour or two.

- Add the rest of the must and wait, taking density readings (remembering to sterilize and rinse the hydrometer before use) until the must attains the same density as when the fermentation stopped. This detail is essential, otherwise the sudden contact with the stronger alcohol content might kill the yeast when it is mixed into the must in the fermentor or carboy.

- Another important precaution is to ascertain that the restarter and the must are the same temperature, so that the inoculation will take place smoothly. If the must has not yet been siphoned into a secondary fermentor, or carboy, this will be easier: simply place the (sterilized) recipient containing the restarter inside the primary fermentor for a while until the respective contents reach a uniform temperature. If the must is in a carboy, the two recipients should preferably be in the same room. A heating belt (available at winemakers' supply stores) can be used to heat the cooler substance until it is the same temperature as the warmer one.

- Finally, the restarter should be poured delicately into the carboy, without stirring. Wait for half an hour, even an hour, before stirring.

If the restarter has been prepared properly, the fermentation should start up again and continue until the must attains the desired density. By restarting the process, you will have rescued 20 or 23 litres of wine from limbo!

We would like to stress that the fermentation lock should be used continually from the beginning of the fermentation process until the bottling stage. Even when the release of gas has finished, changes in temperature may cause the liquid to expand. While the fermentation lock will accomodate this expansion, an air-tight stopper will be forced out, exposing the wine to oxidation.

Making Wine from Concentrated Must

Concentrates have this particularity among the other forms of must available: they require balancing by the winemaker to achieve good results. The winemaker must add several ingredients when reconstituting the must: water, acids, tannin, sugar, clarifier, stabilizer, and occasionally, other additives.

Many amateurs insist on always making their wine with concentrated must, and claim to be entirely satisfied with the results. They have usually found a particular kind of concentrate to their liking, and have remained faithful to it over the years. It is true that some of them do succeed in producing astonishly good wine by this means.

We are including, below, a typical recipe for making wine from concentrated must. The final result is a good quality wine of medium body, with a maturation period of three or four months. We cannot recommend a particular brand of concentrate, both for ethical reasons and because these products may evolve and change due to modifications and improvements in the way the different companies compose and process them. You will have to make your own considered choice, with the advice of your winemaking supply retailer.

Ingredients

- Concentrated must in a 3- or 4-litre (100 oz.) format to produce 19 litres [2] of wine;
- 1.8 kilograms (4 lbs.) of dextrose (sugar appropriate for fermentation purposes);
- a packet of additives (containing tannin, acids, and yeast nutrients). If this is not provided with the concentrate, you will have to obtain an acid titration kit to carry out your own acid balancing;

2. For the equivalents in Imperial and U.S. measures, see page 189.

- a packet of elderberries (150 g./6 oz.) to adjust the colour and enhance the flavour of red wine;
- 15 litres of distilled water, spring water, or tap water (boiled and cooled);
- a packet of stabilizer;
- a packet of potassium metabisulphite crystals ("meta");
- a clarifier;
- metatartric crystals (optional);
- oak chips, or oak flavour essence (optional).

Vinification Method for Concentrated Must

Throughout the following process, remember to note your data (density readings, tastings, additives, etc.) on your winemaking record card.

- If your primary fermentor is not graduated (provided with a built-in scale), use your secondary fermentor, or carboy, to mark the appropriate level on it: fill the carboy with water, pour the contents into the primary fermentor, indicate the level on the fermentor with coloured pencil, then remove the liquid.
- Verify for colour and taste (the concentrated must should have an agreeable flavour, although very sweet). If you have any doubts about the taste, take a sample to your supplier to have it analyzed.
- Pour the concentrate and five litres of hot purified water into the primary fermentor (which has been washed, disinfected, and rinsed thoroughly).
- Add the dextrose and the packet of additives.
- For red wines, tie the elderberries into a cheesecloth or nylon net bag and put them into the must.
- Stir the contents, making sure that the dextrose has completely dissolved.

- If necessary, add purified water until the mixture reaches the level that you had marked on the fermentor (corresponding to the 19-litre capacity of your secondary fermentor, or carboy). The temperature of the must should now be between 20°C and 30°C (68°F - 86°F).
- Take an acidity reading as well as a pH level reading if you have the necessary apparatus [3]; note the results and make any necessary adjustments at this point.
- Take a density reading with the hydrometer: the specific gravity reading should be between 1.080 and 1.090 (to produce an alcohol content between 11% and 12%); take care that the hydrometer and its cylinder are disinfected right before each use by sulphiting them (spraying them with standard metabisulphite solution) and rinsing them with purified water.
- Prepare the yeast, following the directions on the packet.
- When the temperature of the must is between 20°C and 30° (68°F - 86°F), add the yeast.
- Cover the primary fermentor with plastic sheeting (or with its own lid), securing it below the rim with a string attached to an elastic band, a giant-sized elastic band, or bungee cords.
- Let stand to ferment in a warm area without draughts (20°C - 30°C, or 68°F - 86°F); if the room is too cold, put a heating belt (available at your home wine shop) around the vat.
- On the following day, verify that fermentation has actually begun. You should be able to see some froth on the surface, or at least a continuous rising and bursting of bubbles. If you can detect no activity whatsoever, consult your winemaking equipment retailer to determine

---

3. The information concerning acid rates is given in Chapter 3 (page 58); the acid titration kit is described in Chapter 7 (page 201).

whether you should add yeast starter to induce fermentation [4].

- On the sixth day after fermentation has begun, verify the density of the must with the hydrometer (remembering to sulphite and rinse the hydrometer and its cylinder before use).
- If the S.G. reading indicates 1.020 or less, siphon the wine into a secondary fermentor, or carboy, taking care that you have first drained and removed the sack of elderberries. *Carry out a "spread-out" racking to aerate the must*: hold the siphon tube inside the neck of the carboy in such a way that the liquid runs over the inside surface of the carboy. The must will then be efficiently aerated and will release a lot of its carbon dioxide, which keeps the ferment vigorous and healthy.

Inexperienced winemakers tend to leave too much must behind in the primary fermentor when they carry out this first racking, sometimes an inch or an inch and a half of cloudy liquid that contains yeast useful in the next fermentation stage. When transferring the must to the secondary fermentor, tilt the primary fermentor to transfer the maximum amount possible through the siphon tube, and leave only a bare minimum (not more than $1/2$ cup, or 4 ounces) of sediment, or solid particles behind.

- Fill the carboy, leaving at least 5 cm. (2 in.) between the surface of the wine and the bottom of the stopper, or bung, that will be inserted into the neck. If fermentation is still too active (if a lot of froth is visible), the carboy risks overflowing. In that case, leave more leeway at this time (10 cm., or 4 in.) and add some wine (from the same batch) after a day or two to top up the difference.

---

4. See earlier in this chapter for the method of preparing yeast starter and restarter.

If you do not have wine for this purpose, use distilled water or spring water. [5]

- Install the fermentation lock and pour in standard metabisulphite solution [6] to the level indicated; cover the fermentation lock with its cap, which protects the contents from dust and slows evaporation.
- Wash the primary fermentor thoroughly and allow it to dry out completely before putting it away.
- Fermentation should be over by the 21st day. To verify this, take a density reading with the hydrometer (first sulphiting and rinsing both the hydrometer and its cylinder), and write down the result.
- Carry out a second racking, filling the secondary fermentor, or carboy, to within 5 cm. (2 in.) of the bottom of the stopper in the neck. In this racking, keep air exposure to a minimum by holding the end of the siphon at the bottom of the carboy instead of directing the flow onto its inner surface.

Bulk Aging, or Cuvaison

- Allow the wine to stand for one month. Verify the density: the specific gravity should be 0.995 or less for dry wines, and 0.998 for sweeter wines. If the density is still above 1.000, prolong the fermentation for a few days. If the S.G. reading is till too high, consult your retailer to determine if fermentation has to be induced again with restarter [7].

---

5. It is much preferable to add wine. However, the addition of 5 % water to the must (one litre, in this case) is acceptable.
6. Standard metabisulphite solution is made from 50g. (9 level, not heaping, teaspoons) of potassium metabisulphite crystals dissolved in 4 litres (about a gallon) of lukewarm water.
7. For the preparation of yeast starter and restarter, see the beginning of this chapter.

- Smell and taste your wine. If the vinification process has been successful, it should taste like young ("raw") wine at this point.
- Add clarifier, or fining (isinglass) to clear the wine; potassium metabisulphite may be included in the same packet.
- If the metabisulphite crystals are not included with the other additives, dissolve one level quarter-teaspoon of it in lukewarm water and stir it into the wine.
- Add the stabilizer, dissolved in 60 ml. (^{1}/4 cup) of luke-warm water (the metabisulphite may be contained in the same packet).
- Add metatartric acid if you dislike the presence of tar-trate deposits, or wine "crystals" in your bottles of wine. Another way to prevent this is to cool the must to 0°C - 4°C (32°F - 39°F) for two or three weeks (some wine-makers leave their carboys outside in cool or cold weather for this reason, but the wine should not be allowed to freeze). Any crystals will now have formed and will be easy to remove before bottling. (However, remember that transporting the carboys is always risky.) If you have a second refrigerator, it can be used for this purpose.
- If you like, add oak flavour essence at this stage.
- You may also add sweetners if you wish to sweeten your wine.

Bottling and Aging

- One month later, filter your wine. If you do not own a filtering system, you can rent one from your wine-making equipment dealer. Filtering is rather a long operation, but it produces excellent results: the wine becomes perfectly clear and has an agreeable consisten-cy for drinking. Moreover, if the particles that form the lees are not filtered out, they may prejudice the wine's flavour.

- Bottle your wine; if you do not own a corking machine, you can rent this useful piece of equipment. Allow the bottles to stand upright for ten days.
- Let the wine age for at least three months before tasting it.
- The wine will be better if allowed to age for one year; it can be preserved for two or three years, after which it will begin to lose its qualities and spoil.

Primary Fermentation

- Pour the concentrate into the primary fermentor.
- Add the accompanying manufacturer's ingredients.
- Add water and adjust temperature.
- Take an initial S.G. (density) reading.
- Add yeast.
- Cover with lid or plastic sheeting.
- Leave to ferment at a temperature of 20-30°C (68-86°F).

Day 0 - 6

Secondary Fermentation

- At a S.G. reading of 1.020, rack into the secondary fermentor.
- Fill, leaving 5 cm. (2 in.) leeway under the bottom of the stopper.
- Install the fermentation lock and pour standard metabisulphite solution into it.
- Rack on the 21st day.

Day 7 to 21

Bulk Aging, or *Cuvaison*

- Let stand 1 month in carboy.
- At a S.G. of 0.995 (dry wine) or 0.998 (sweet wine), fermentation is finished.
- Add stabilizer, clarifier, metatartric crystals and other improving agents.
- Add metabisulphite (if necessary).

Day 22 to 52
(1 month)

Maturation

- Add sweeteners (to taste).
- Wait 1 month and filter.
- Bottle your wine.
- Age for at least 3 months.
- The wine will improve after 1 year of aging.

Day 53 to 83
(1 month)

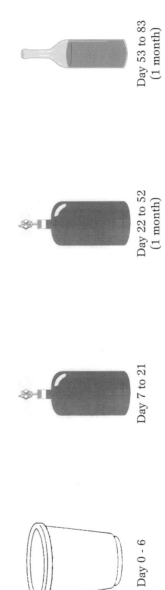

Chart 1. Summary of Winemaking with Concentrated Must

Making wine with the 28-Day Concentrate Kit

The advantage of kits is that they come with everything the amateur needs to make wine from concentrated must "in 28 days". With a kit, nothing will be missing at the last minute, and there is an additional sense of security in knowing that all the products included have been laboratory-tested and are compatible with the must that will be made into wine. Moreover, they are pH-balanced, which means one less tricky operation that has to be carried out by the winemaker. In general, the concentrated musts contain invert sugar which helps the wine attain a desirable alcohol rate.

The formats of the kits vary: the most usual are 5, 8, and 15 litres [8]. The difference between them lies in the degrees of concentration and the proportion of sterilized must that may have been added to the concentrate.

Some kits offer a variety of strongly concentrated musts (in a proportion of 4.5 to 1, that is, 4.5 litres of must has been reduced to 1 litre of concentrate), while others offer musts that are not as strongly concentrated. The 15-litre format contains a certain proportion of sterilized must, depending on the brand. These mixtures of concentrated and sterilized must produce better-quality wines than simple concentrates.

These days, the vast majority of home winemakers who want a wine that can be drunk young prefer to buy a concentrate kit instead of concentrate by itself.

Note that most of the kits are designed to produce 23 litres of wine. Make sure that you have carboys of the appropriate capacity to be able to carry out the winemaking process smoothly.

---

8. For the equivalents in Imperial and U.S. measures, see page 189.

Ingredients (Usually Included)

- Concentrated must in a 5-, 8-, or 15-litre format;
- a packet of bentonite;
- a packet of additives (containing the tannin and the acids); in some kits, the additives have already been dissolved in the concentrate;
- a packet of yeast;
- a stabilizer containing potassium metabisulphite;
- a clarifier (optional);
- metatartric acid (optional);
- oak chips, or oak flavour essence (optional).

Vinification Method for the 28-Day Kit

Throughout the following process, remember to note your data (density readings, tastings, additives, etc.) on your winemaking record card.

- Taste the concentrate and verify its colour. A good-quality concentrate will have a pleasant taste, although it is very sweet. If it has a doubtful taste, take a sample to your retailer for analysis.
- Pour the concentrate into the primary fermentor which has been washed, disinfected, and well rinsed with purified water.
- Add the packet of additives and stir until the mixture has a uniform consistency.
- Add the amount of purified water necessary to make 23 litres of reconstituted must, taking care to keep the temperature of the must between 20°C and 30°C (68°F - 86°F).
- In some kits, the bentonite has to be added at this point, whereas in other kits, it is added on Day 6. In either case, the bentonite should be very thoroughly

mixed with purified water first (see Chapter 7, page 189).

- Add oak chips, if desired. They must be sterilized first by heating them for 20 minutes in the oven at 90°C - 100°C (194°F - 212°F), but no hotter or they may acquire a burnt taste. The oak chips can be added during either the primary or the secondary fermentation stage. Follow the directions included in the kit; it is usually recommended to put the chips into a cheesecloth or a nylon-net sachet, with one or two sterilized glass marbles in it to keep it down at the bottom of the fermentor or carboy. It can be left in the carboy for two months. Oak flavour essence, on the other hand, can be added right before the filtration process.
- Take a density reading with the hydrometer: the specific gravity reading should be between 1.080 and 1.090 (to produce an alcohol strength between 11% and 12%); take care that the hydrometer and its cylinder are disinfected immediately before each use (by spraying with standard metabisulphite solution and rinsing with purified water).
- Prepare the yeast, following the directions on the packet.
- When the temperature of the must is between 20°C and 30°C (68°F - 86°F), add the yeast.
- Cover the primary fermentor with plastic sheeting (or with its own lid), securing it below the rim either with a string attached to an elastic band, or with a giant-sized elastic band.
- Let stand to ferment in a warm area without drafts (20°C - 30°C, or 68°F - 86°F); if the room is too cold, put a heating belt (available at your home wine shop) around the vat.
- On the following day, verify that fermentation has actually started. You should be able to see some froth on the surface, or at least a continuous rising and bursting of bubbles. If you can detect no activity whatsoever, seek

advice from your winemaking supplier to determine whether yeast starter is necessary[9].

- On the sixth day after fermentation has begun (primary fermentation can last up to ten days), verify the density of the must with the hydrometer. If the specific gravity is 1.020 or less, prepare a 23-litre secondary fermentor, or carboy, by washing, disinfecting, and rinsing it with purified water. Always remember that the hydrometer and its cylinder should be disinfected before each use.

- Pour the bentonite mixed with water into the carboy, if this has not already been done (see above).

When an additive is mixed into must which is still in ferment, or has just ceased fermenting, the remaining carbon dioxide imprisoned in it will be violently released, producing a volcano effect, and a good part of the must will be lost. To prevent this, the additive can be put at the bottom of the secondary fermentor; the must will release the carbon dioxide as it is racked over it and any violent bubbling will be contained within the recipient.

- Siphon the wine into the secondary fermentor, or carboy, leaving only a few ounces of sediment in the primary fermentor; tilt the primary fermentor to draw off as much of the must as possible. Carry out a "spread-out" racking to aerate the must: direct the flow of the wine so that it spreads out onto the inside surface of the carboy. The wine will be oxygenized just enough, and will release a lot of its carbon dioxide, which helps maintain a vigorous and healthy ferment. Fill the carboy, leaving at least 5 cm. (2 in.) between the surface of the wine and the bottom of the stopper, or bung, that will be inserted into the neck, unless too much fermentation is still going on (if there is

---

9. To prepare the yeast starter, refer to the beginning of this chapter (page 123).

still a lot of frothing), and the carboy risks overflowing. If this is the case, leave more leeway at this time (10 cm., or 4 in.) and top it up with some wine (from the same batch) in a day or two to make up the difference. If you do not have the wine for this purpose, use distilled water or spring water [10].

- Install the fermentation lock and pour in standard metabisulphite solution [11] to the level indicated; cork the fermentation lock and cover it with its cap, which protects the contents from dust and slows evaporation.

Bulk Aging, or Cuvaison

- Fermentation should be over by the 21st day.
- Verify the density: if the specific gravity has decreased to 0.995 or less for dry wines, and 0.998 for sweeter wines, add the stabilizer and clarifier.
- If the density is still above the required norm, prolong the fermentation until the desired density is reached. If necessary, place the carboy in a warmer place to activate the ferment. Above all, do not bottle the wine until it attains the right density.
- If the S.G. reading continues to be too high, consult your retailer to determine if fermentation has to be induced again with restarter [12].
- Add metatartric acid if you dislike the presence of tartrate deposits or wine "crystals" in your bottles of wine. A method of removing the crystals before bottling is to cool the must to 0°C - 4°C (32°F - 39°F) for two or

10. It is much preferable to add wine. However, the addition of 5% water to the must (about one litre, or a quart, in this case) is acceptable.
11. Standard metabisulphite solution is made from 50g. (9 level, not heaping, teaspoons) of potassium metabisulphite crystals, dissolved in 4 litres (about a gallon) of lukewarm water.
12. For the preparation of restarter, see the beginning of this chapter (page 125).

three weeks, after which the crystals will have formed. Some winemakers leave their carboys outside for this purpose when the weather is cold enough (watch that the wine doesn't freeze!) (However, remember that transporting the carboys is always risky.). If you have a second refrigerator, it can be used for this purpose.

- Add the clarifier or fining (isinglass); the potassium metabisulphite may be contained in one of the packets provided by the producer.
- If it is not already included in one of the packets containing the additives, dissolve one level quarter-teaspoon of potassium metabisulphite crystals in a little water and add it to the wine.
- Add the stabilizer.
- If you like, add oak flavour essence at this stage.
- You may add sweeteners if you wish to sweeten your wine.

Bottling and Aging

- On the 28th day, filter your wine (if it is not clear, let stand for a few more days). If you do not own a filtering system, you can rent one from your winemaking equipment dealer. Filtering is a rather lengthy operation, but it produces excellent results: the wine becomes perfectly clear and agreeable to drink. Moreover, filtering removes the dead yeast cells (the lees) which may impair the wine's flavour if left in the bottle for several months.
- Bottle your wine; if you do not own a corking machine, you can rent this useful piece of equipment. Allow the bottles to stand upright for ten days.
- Let the wine age at least two months before tasting it.
- The wine will be better if allowed to age for one year; it can be preserved for three or four years, after which it will begin to deteriorate.

Primary Fermentation

- Pour the concentrate into the primary fermentor.
- Mix in additives.
- Add water and adjust temperature.
- Take an initial S.G. (density) reading.
- Add yeast.
- Cover with lid or plastic sheeting.
- Ferment at a temperature of 20-24°C (68-86°F).

Secondary Fermentation

- At a S.G. reading of 1.020, add bentonite if not already done.
- Rack (siphon) into the secondary fermentor.
- Fill, leaving 5 cm. (2 in.) leeway under the bottom of the stopper, or bung.
- Install the fermentation lock and pour standard metabisulphite solution into it.

Bulk Aging, or *Cuvaison*

- Wait until the 21st day.
- At a S.G. of 0.995 (dry wine) or 0.998 (sweet wine), fermentation is over.
- Add stabilizer, clarifier, metatartric crystals and other improving agents.
- Add metabisulphite (if it was not already included in the packets of other ingredients).
- Add sweeteners (to taste).

Maturation

- Wait 7 days and filter.
- Bottle your wine.
- Age for at least 3 months.
- The wine will improve after 1 year of aging.

Day 0 - 6

Day 7 to 20

Day 21 to 28

Day 28

Chart 2. Summary of Winemaking with a 28-Day Concentrate Kit

Making Wine from Sterilized Must

Sterilized (or pasteurized) musts have been available on the market for a few years now, largely due to innovations by the Mosti Mondiale company. This format is coming into its own as home winemakers discover that it often produces better results than concentrate does. When purchased, sterilized musts have already been fully prepared for the winemaking process, and the amateur has almost nothing to do but patiently wait for the wine to mature!

These musts are usually 100% pure. It is possible to buy sterilized must composed solely of noble grape varieties such as Cabernet Sauvignon, Merlot, Chardonnay, Riesling, and others. There are also high-quality blends available which produce excellent wines.

All things considered, the arrival of sterilized musts on the market has been a blessing for home winemakers. The one cloud on the horizon is the fact that some producers are selling "sterilized" or "pasteurized" musts which are in fact reconstituted from concentrates. This means that the manufacturer has simply bought concentrated must and added water (which you could do yourself), then sold the result as if it were 100% pure.

A few must producers sell a combination of the two, that is, pure must mixed with reconstituted concentrate. Obviously, you should read the labels carefully to know exactly what you are buying in this domain. Why should you pay a higher price when the product is just a concentrate with the water added?

We reiterate that these pure musts (if they really are pure!) will not undergo malolactic fermentation for the simple reason that they have been sterilized: all the bacteria in them have been killed, including the malolactic bacteria.

A last point: read the directions that come with the sterilized must attentively, and if something is not clear to you (we have noticed that a few of these companies are masters in the art of confusion!), you had better consult your retailer, who will give you all the information you need to carry out the procedures properly.

The most common packaging for sterilized must is a sealed plastic bag containing the must, inside a plastic bucket with a capacity of 25 litres, the minimum size required to ferment that particular quantity of must. Therefore, the risk of overflow is high, and we suggest that you either use a larger primary fermentor, or take measures to protect your floor or carpet.

It is better not to attempt pouring the must directly from the bag into the fermentor: you may end up with more on the floor than in the recipient. These bags are very flexible and there is no proper way to get a grip on them; it is difficult to prevent the must from shooting out in all directions. You should siphon the must into the fermentor, or at least the first third of it. After that, it will be easier to manipulate the bag and there will be less risk of wasting the must and staining everything on or near you.

It is important to note down the lot number of the sterilized or pasteurized must. If there is one, it will either be on the bag itself or on the stopper. This number constitutes your guarantee, at least in the case of reputable must suppliers.

We also suggest that you taste the must at this point. Whether it is red or white, it should have a pleasant, sweet taste. If you are in any doubt about its taste, you should take a sample to show your retailer, before it is too late.

At the same time, verify the colour of the must. It should either be dark red (not at all brownish), or clear with an amber hue (especially not brownish, or dark caramel) in the case of white must.

You might verify whether the producer has been kind enough to provide a "best before" or expiry date on the container. Not many companies do this, which is unfortunate, as sterilized must only stays fresh for a period varying from 12 to 18 months.

Ingredients (Usually Packaged Together)

- 23 litres of pasteurized must in a sealed bag within a plastic bucket;
- a packet of bentonite;
- a packet of yeast;
- a packet of additives (containing tannin and acids); note that the additives are sometimes already dissolved in the must;
- a stabilizer containing potassium metabisulphite;
- clarifier (optional);
- oak chips or oak flavour essence (optional).

Vinification Method for Sterilized Must

Throughout the following process, remember to note your data (density readings, tastings, additives, etc.) on your winemaking record card.

- Pour the pasteurized must into the primary fermentor (which has been washed, disinfected, and rinsed with water).
- Add the bentonite mixed with purified water, if this is specified in the directions. This operation is necessary to clear wine intended for drinking very young; it is unnecessary for winemakers who are willing to wait a few months before drinking their wine.
- Verify the temperature: it should be between 20°C and 30°C (68°F - 86°F).
- Take a density reading with the hydrometer and note down the result: the specific gravity reading should be between 1.080 and 1.090 (to produce an alcohol content between 11% and 12% or 22-24 proof); take care that the hydrometer and the cylinder are disinfected right before use ("sulphite" or spray with standard

metabisulphite solution and rinse with purified water).

- Prepare the yeast, following the directions on the packet.
- When the temperature of the must is between 20°C and 30° (68°F - 86°F), add the yeast. Let stand for half an hour, then stir.
- Cover the primary fermentor with plastic sheeting (or with its own lid), securing it below the rim with a string attached to an elastic band or simply use one giant-size elastic band.
- Let stand to ferment in a warm area without draughts (20°C - 30°C, or 68°F - 86°F); if the room is too cold, put a heating belt (available at your winemakers' supply shop) around the fermentor.
- On the following day, verify that fermentation has effectively begun. You should be able to see some froth on the surface, or at least a continuous rising and bursting of bubbles. If you detect no activity whatsoever, seek advice from your winemaking retailer to determine whether using yeast starter is necessary [13].
- On the sixth day after primary fermentation has started (this stage can last up to ten days), verify the density of the must with the hydrometer. Don't forget that the hydrometer and its cylinder must be disinfected and rinsed with purified water before each use. If the hydrometer indicates a specific gravity of 1.020 or less, prepare a 23-litre (approximately 5 gallons) secondary fermentor, or carboy, washed, disinfected, and rinsed with purified water.
- Siphon the wine into the secondary fermentor (or carboy). Leave only a few ounces of sediment behind, to ensure that enough yeast is transferred into the secondary fermentor; tilt the primary fermentor when

13. To prepare yeast starter, see the beginning of this chapter (page 123).

Sediment visible in a carboy
of white wine.

racking to draw off as much of the must as possible. Carry out a "spread-out" racking to aerate the must: hold the tube end in the neck of the carboy in such a way that the wine spreads over the inside surface of the carboy; the wine will be oxygenized just enough, and release a lot of its carbon dioxide, which will keep the ferment healthy and vigorous.

• Fill the carboy, leaving at least 5 cm. (2 in.) between the surface of the wine and the bottom of the stopper, or bung, that will be inserted into the neck, unless too much fermentation is still going on (if there is a lot of frothing), and the carboy risks overflowing. If this is the case, leave more leeway at this time (10 cm. or 4 in.) then top up with some wine (from the same batch) in a day or two to make up the difference. If you do not have wine for this purpose, use distilled water or spring water [14].

• Install the fermentation lock and pour in standard metabisulphite solution [15] to the level indicated; cork the fermentation lock and cover it with its cap, which protects the contents from dust and slows evaporation.

---

14. It is much preferable to add wine. However, the addition of 5% purified water (one litre, or about one quart, in this case) is acceptable.

15. Standard metabisulphite solution is made from 50g. (9 level, not heaping, teaspoons) of potassium metabisulphite crystals, dissolved in 4 litres (about a gallon) of lukewarm water.

Bulk Aging, or **Cuvaison**

- Some sterilized must producers recommend racking again after ten days; if this is the case, proceed with a normal racking.
- Fermentation should have ceased by the 21st day.
- Verify the density: the specific gravity should have decreased to about 0.995 or less for dry wines, and to 0.998 for sweeter wines. Don't forget to sulphite and rinse the apparatus when carrying out hydrometer readings.
- If the density is still above 0.995 or above 0.998 (for dry and sweeter wines respectively), prolong the fermentation until the must attains the required density. If necessary, place the carboy in a warmer place to invigorate the fermentation process. If the S.G. reading continues to be too high, consult your retailer to determine if fermentation has to be induced again with restarter [16].
- Proceed with the second racking (or the third, if you did a second racking after 10 days, as mentioned above). If you do not have another carboy for this, you can use your primary fermentor, after disinfecting and rinsing it. Siphon the wine into the recipient as quickly as possible to avoid any unnecessary contact with the air, then siphon it back into the secondary fermentor which has been sanitized, or sulphited, in the meantime.
- Add metatartric acid to prevent the formation of tartrate deposits, if you do not want any in your wine once it is bottled. Alternatively, you can also remove them easily by cooling the must to 0°C - 4°C (32°F - 39°F) for two or three weeks. Some winemakers leave the carboy outside in the cold for this purpose (without allowing the wine to actually freeze). (Remember, however,

---

16. For the preparation of restarter, see earlier in this chapter (page 125).

that transporting the carboys is risky.) If you have a second refrigerator, it can be used for this purpose.

- Add the clarifier or fining (isinglass); the potassium metabisulphite may be contained in one of the packets provided by the producer.
- If it is not already included in one of the packets containing the additives, dissolve one level quarter-teaspoon of potassium metabisulphite crystals in a little water and add it to the wine.
- Add the stabilizer.
- You may add sweeteners if you want to sweeten your wine.

Your kit may include oak chips. Please follow manufacturers' instructions.

Bottling and Aging

- On the 28th day, filter your wine. If you do not own a filtering system, you can rent one from your wine-making equipment dealer. Filtering can be a rather lengthy operation, but it produces excellent results: the wine becomes perfectly clear and pleasant to drink. Moreover, the dead yeast cells that form the lees may prejudice the wine's flavour if they are left in the bottle for several months; filtering will eliminate this risk.
- Bottle your wine; if you do not own a corking machine, you can rent this useful piece of equipment. Allow the bottles to stand upright for ten days.
- Let the wine age for three months before drinking it.
- The wine will be better if allowed to age in the bottles for one year; it will keep all of its flavour up to three to five years, after which it will begin to lose its qualities and spoil.

Primary Fermentation

- Pour the sterilized must into the primary fermentor.
- Add the accompanying manufacturer's ingredients, with bentonite if the wine is to be drunk very young.
- Take an initial S.G. (density) reading.
- Add the yeast.
- Cover with lid or plastic sheeting.
- Ferment at a temperature of 20-30°C (68-86°F).

Secondary Fermentation

- At a S.G. reading of 1.020, rack into a secondary fermentor.
- Leave 5 cm. (2 in.) leeway between the wine and the bottom of the stopper.
- Install the fermentation lock and pour standard metabisulphite solution into it.

Bulk Aging, or *Cuvaison*

- Wait until the 20th day.
- At a S.G. of 0.995 (dry wine) or 0.998 (sweet wine), fermentation is over. Rack.
- Add stabilizer, fining, metatartric crystals and other improving agents (and potassium metabisulphite, if it was not already included with the other ingredients).
- Add sweeteners (optional).

Maturation

- On the 28th day, filter your wine.
- Bottle your wine.
- Age for at least 3 months.
- The wine will improve with 1 year of aging.

Day 0 - 6

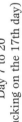

Day 7 to 20
(racking on the 17th day)

Day 21 to 28

Day 28

Chart 3. Summary of Winemaking with Sterilized Must

Making Wine from Fresh Must

Some producers offer fresh musts that are blended and packaged right after the grapes are harvested. These musts have not been sterilized, but their acidity is balanced before they are distributed for sale. They are kept refrigerated at a temperature between -2°C and -4°C (25°F - 28°F), that is, a temperature at which the must will keep fresh but not freeze hard.

Fresh musts come in formats of 20- and 23-litre pails and in 100-litre barrels. They are not usually sold in winemakers' shops, as very few retailers have the refrigeration facilities necessary to prevent the fresh musts from starting to ferment (selected yeasts have already been added to them).

Thus, the amateur winemaker must order the fresh must, which will be delivered on a specific day.

However, depending on the volume of the demand, some winemaking supply retailers rent refrigerated delivery trucks during the high season to be able to satisfy their ever-growing clientele. A few of them have invested in large refrigeration facilities that can store several hundred orders of must; some retailers can even hold musts made from particular grape varieties in reserve for customers who have requested them.

Nearly all the available fresh musts are made up of classic and semi-classic grape varieties from California, Italy, Spain, and other European countries. Their prices are generally lower than those of sterilized musts, simply because they have not undergone the relatively costly pasteurization process.

Fresh musts are kept on the market until the supply is exhausted; some types of fresh must sell out immediately, while others are available for more than six months, or even throughout the year.

A new supply of fresh musts arrive in the spring, from southern hemisphere countries where the growing season is the reverse of our own. These fresh musts come from Chile, Argentina, and Australia.

The fickle nature of the grape occasionally leads to surprises. In a particular year, Pinot Noir musts may have produced magnificent wines, whereas that season's Cabernet Sauvignon crop was rather disappointing. However, all the wine produced from these musts are excellent, and are almost always superior to those made from concentrates or sterilized musts. The reason is very simple: they are much purer. The very slight modifications that they undergo are limited to balancing their acidity, adjusting their colour, and adding metabisulphite for preservation purposes. These fresh musts contain their natural water, and have kept their microflora intact, all of which results in wines with a good nose.

Wines made from good-quality fresh must always have more flavour than those made from sterilized must; this is quite obvious at first sip.

As we have already mentioned, it is very important to read the labels on the must containers carefully. Some companies are passing off reconstituted concentrates as "fresh must." We warn you again against falling victim to this kind of dubious practice.

In the same vein, we must point out that not all fresh musts produce marvellous wines. A poor-quality fresh must is obviously not better than, nor equal to a high-quality sterilized must. The quality of the grape variety counts more than the processing that the must has undergone, so that certain kinds of sterilized must and even some concentrated musts may be far superior to a fresh must made from a third-rate grape variety, or from grapes in bad condition.

Be this as it may, fresh musts for winemaking are very successful these days, mostly because they are selected where the grapes are grown and when they are at their peak ripeness. This is clearly better than making wine from grapes that are shipped when still unripe (so they won't spoil); these grapes are usually lacking in sugar, have too much tannin, and are very acidic. Moreover, they are often classified according to the whims of the vendor. Only a very experienced expert can tell a Cabernet Sauvignon grape from its Cabernet Franc cousin at first glance. Even the specialists occasionally fail to distinguish one variety from another when they resemble each other closely. We will return to this subject in the following section (on winemaking using whole grapes).

We should mention, finally, that the Mosti Mondiale company offers home winemakers the possibility of a compromise between using fresh refrigerated must and whole grapes. Their "Sonoma edition" comes in the same format as the refrigerated musts, with the bonus that the must in the 23-litre bucket contains an additional two kilos (5 lbs.) of grapeskins, thus allowing the home winemaker to pigment his or her own red wine (and to increase the tannin content).

Mosti Mondiale also offers amateur winemakers a seasonal selection of fresh musts made from classic and semi-classic grape varieties. Imported from France and Italy, the grapes of this "Harvest Collection" issue are picked when ripe, destemmed, crushed, frozen, and sold in 20- and 23-litre plastic pails. The winemaker should treat this limited-edition must with the same methods used for making wine from whole grapes. The essential information for the winemaking process is provided, that is, the pH level, the total acidity rate, the density (Brix scale), and the amount of metabisulphite contained in the must. This experience is still in a trial phase; the "Harvest Collection" was available in restricted quantities in the autumn of 1997.

Ingredients

- Fresh refrigerated must in a 20- or 23-litre capacity container. Fresh must can only be obtained by ordering it from the supplier. It should be maintained at a temperature of -2°C (25°F). If the winemaker has waited too long before picking up the order, the must may already have started to ferment.

The recipe given below applies to a red wine for which malolactic fermentation is desired. The recipe for white wine follows it.

Vinification Method for Fresh Red Must

Throughout the following process, remember to note your data (density readings, tastings, additives, etc.) on your winemaking record card.

- Allow the fresh must to lose its chill at a room temperature of 20°C - 30°C (68°F - 86°F) or heat the container with a heating belt (available at winemakers' supply shops). Make sure that the container has an escape valve: as soon as fermentation begins, there is a risk that the must will overflow, or blow the lid off. The producer may have punched a little hole in the lid to allow any excess pressure or froth to escape at the beginning of fermentation.
- If the must was refrigerated several weeks after it was made (if it was bought in January, for example), we suggest using the same type of yeast that inoculated it when it was packaged. You can also try other yeasts according to your needs, whether it be a D47-type yeast that encourages malolactic fermentation, or a Burgundy-type yeast if you are aiming for this type of wine, etc. Always follow the maker's directions on the yeast packet to the letter.
- As soon as the must has thawed out, siphon it into the appropriate-sized primary fermentor. If siphoning is too difficult because of the gas given off by the ferment, pour the must into the primary fermentor (which has been washed, disinfected, and rinsed with purified water). Note that you can leave the must to ferment in its container; however, make sure that the floors and

other objects near it are well protected, as the manufacturer's container leaves only the bare minimum space required for the must to ferment.

- Take a density reading with the hydrometer. Remember the importance of sterilizing the hydrometer and its cylinder before every use (by sulphiting and rinsing thoroughly with purified water). Write down the specific gravity reading obtained. It should be between 1.080 and 1.095 (to obtain an alcohol content between 11% and 12.5%). You can also ask your retailer if he or she has the list of the initial density readings of the musts when they were prepared and packaged; some distributors include these lists with the musts that they deliver to retail outlets. If you can obtain this initial reading, note it down with the other readings on your winemaking record card.

- Taste the must: whether it is a white or red must, it should have a pleasant, sweet taste, as well as an agreeable smell. If it doesn't, you had better take a sample to your retailer right away. Be careful that your sample does not overflow: it will be in full ferment at this stage. Use a large enough recipient and carry it in a well-closed plastic bag.

- Verify the colour of the must as well. This should be done as early as possible, because once fermentation is under way, red must will take on a greyish-pink colour and white must will become milky.

- When you have ascertained that the must is in good condition, cover the primary fermentor with plastic sheeting (or its own lid), tying it down around the rim with string or cord attached to an elastic band or a giant-sized elastic band.

- Let stand to ferment in a warm room without draughts (at 20°C - 30°C, or 68°F - 86°F). If the room is too cold, warm the must with a heating belt (available at the winemaking equipment shop). If malolactic fermentation is desired in the case of red wines, this temperature must be maintained for three months. A heating belt will certainly be necessary if the must is left to ferment in an unheated basement.

- Fermentation is usually very active and bubbly for the first ten days, but this is not the case for all types of must: some produce less froth than others. It is better to verify with the hydrometer, which will tell you exactly how fermentation is progressing.

- After a period varying between five and seven days (although this can take as long as ten days), the hydrometer should indicate a specific gravity reading of 1.020 or less. (Remember to sterilize and rinse the hydrometer with purified water before every reading, and to log the readings on your winemaking record card for future reference.)

- If the density is low enough, siphon the must into the secondary fermentor, or carboy (which has been disinfected and rinsed with purified water). Transfer as much of the must as possible from the primary fermentor, tilting it if necessary, to avoid wasting must and useful yeast cells. Insert the tube-end through the carboy neck in such a way that the must will spread out over the innner sides of the carboy, thus allowing it to aerate as much as possible. It will be oxygenized just enough, and release a large amount of carbon dioxide, which keeps the ferment vigorous.

- Fill the secondary fermentor, preferably a glass carboy, leaving a 5-cm. (2-inch) leeway under the bottom of the stopper, or bung. If, however, fermentation is still very active (that is, if you see a lot of frothing on the surface), leave a leeway of 10 cm. (4 in.) at this time, and top up the must to the normal level one or two days later with wine (from the same batch). In this recipe, it is preferable not to use water for this purpose.

- We strongly recommend that you use glass carboys when making wine from fresh must. In this method, the wine will remain in the carboy for more than three months, which is enough time for oxygen to penetrate into the must if plastic containers are used. If you have too much wine to go into the carboy(s), you can put it into jars or jugs which can accomodate fermentation locks.

- Install the fermentation lock and pour standard meta solution [17] into it, to the indicated level. Cork the lock and close it with its cap to keep out dust and reduce evaporation.

Bulk Aging, or Cuvaison

- On the 21st day after the beginning of fermentation, the process should be finished (although this can take up to a month). Take a density reading and note it down: it should now be 0.995 (for dry wines) or 0.998 (for sweeter wines).
- If the density is still too high (over 0.995 or 0.998 for dry and sweeter wines respectively), prolong the fermentation process until the required specific gravity reading is obtained. This may necessitate putting the carboy in a warmer place to activate the process. If there is no activity, consult your supplier to determine whether you should use restarter [18].
- Carry out a taste trial. If the wine has a sulphur or rotten egg odour, you should immediately take measures to remedy the situation: add one level quarter-teaspoon of dissolved metabisulphite. Then siphon the wine three of four times into fermentor pails to aerate it and to

---

17. "Standard metabisulphite solution" means 50g. (9 level, not heaping, teaspoons) of potassium metabisulphite crystals dissolved in 4 litres (about a gallon) of lukewarm water.
18. For the preparation of restarter, see the beginning of this chapter (page 125).

eliminate the sulphur odour. Be sure to advise your retailer of the measures you have taken.

- Rack the wine. If you do not have a second carboy, you can use the (sanitized) primary fermentor to hold the wine while you thoroughly clean the carboy. Siphon the wine back into it quickly to prevent too much air contact.
- Apply the fermentation lock, with the appropriate amount of standard metabisulphite solution inside it.
- Leave the wine in the carboy for two or three months at a stable temperature between 20°C and 30°C (68°F - 86°F).
- Verify whether malolactic fermentation has begun. If it has, you should see little bubbles rising continuously, and there will be visible activity inside the fermentation lock.
- If you are using several carboys and only some of them show malolactic fermentation activity, extract 100 ml. (3 fl. oz.) of must from a carboy in which ferment is occurring, and introduce it into the carboy(s) in which there is no perceptible action, to induce malolactic fermentation in them.
- Rack according to the usual method, every four or six weeks as long as you continue to see sediment in your wine.
- After two months, take a density reading, and verify the wine's taste and clarity to make sure everything is going well. If the malolactic fermentation stage has not taken place, the wine must be kept in the carboy(s) for another month at the appropriate temperature, and it may be necessary to use malolactic bacteria (bought from your retailer) to induce malolactic fermentation.
- When the malolactic fermentation stage is finished, activity in the fermentation lock will have ceased. Add one level quarter-teaspoon of metabisulphite dissolved in water to each 20- or 23-litre carboy.
- You may now add oak chips if you want your wine to have an oak cask flavour. The chips must first be sterilized: keep them in the oven for twenty minutes at a

temperature of 90°C - 100°C (194°F - 212°F) but no higher or they may acquire a burnt taste. Secure them in a cleesecloth or nylon net bag with a couple of (sterilized) glass marbles to hold them down at the bottom of the carboy. Oak flavour essence, on the other hand, can be added right before the filtration process.

- At this point, you must make a choice: you can either age your wine in the carboy(s) for a period of nine months starting from the first day of fermentation (and thus avoid the temptation of drinking the wine too young!) or you can proceed with bottling immediately, following the steps outlined below.

The following optional procedures should be carried out in the order in which they are given below:

- Add metatartric acid if you are really opposed to the presence of the harmless tartrate "diamonds" that may collect at the bottom of the bottle. Another way to eliminate these before bottling is to keep the carboy at a low temperature (0°C or 32°F) for two or three weeks during the bulk aging stage; the crystals will form and are easily removed. Some winemakers take advantage of our cold climate and leave their carboys outside, but be careful that the wine doesn't freeze hard! (Its freezing point is a little colder than the freezing point of water.) This technique also incurs greater risk to carboys because of the additional handling. If, on the other hand, you have a second refrigerator, it can be used for this purpose.

- Stabilize your wine with 2 teaspoons of potassium sorbate diluted in $1/4$ cup of purified water, for each 20 or 23 litres of wine. When wine has undergone malolactic fermentation, the potassium sorbate stabilizer cannot be added unless the wine has been sterilized with a level quarter-teaspoon of potassium metabisulphite (for 20 or 23 litres of wine) three days beforehand. This can be done easily by dissolving the metabisulphite crystals in 50 ml. (1 $2/3$ fl. oz.) of lukewarm water, and stirring it vigorously into the wine. Note that if there are sediment deposits at this time, racking should be done.

Treating the wine with metabisulphite three days before stabilizing it is a proven and effective method which almost infallibly prevents your wine from acquiring a geranium odour and becoming undrinkable. The stabilizer prevents the unwanted reoccurrence of fermentation once the wine has been bottled. If this happens, be prepared to drink semi-sparkling wine, or to be woken up in the night by the sound of exploding corks!

- When stabilization has been carried out, clear the wine with isinglass fining, or with bentonite if the wine is cloudy. This operation is optional if you are planning to filter the wine.
- Add sweeteners if you like (to taste).

Bottling and Aging

- One month later, the wine can be filtered. If you do not own filtering equipment, it can be rented from your winemaking equipment shop. This operation is rather long, but the results are excellent: the wine becomes brilliantly clear and has a pleasing consistency for drinking. Moreover, it prevents the lees from giving the wine a bad taste when it is aged for several months.
- Bottle the wine; if you do not own a corking machine, you can rent this useful piece of equipment. Allow the bottles to stand up right for ten days.
- Drink your red wine one year after the beginning of fermentation, and never before three months after bottling [19].

---

19. When it is bottled, wine undergoes a shock that destabilizes it. The three-month period is necessary for it to become balanced again. Regarding aging, see the Wine Maturation Graph in Chapter 5 (page 117).

It can be drunk before this, but it is really not recommended. Wine made from fresh must will improve over a period of three or four years; it will keep easily for five or six years, and even for ten years if kept in a coldroom or cellar.

Vinification Method for Fresh White Must

The vinification process for fresh must made from white grapes is almost the same as that for red must, except that malolactic fermentation is not desired, as it would produce a flat white wine.

However, in the exceptional case of Chardonnay must, we advise carrying out exactly the same procedure as when making wine from red musts, including the malolactic fermentation stage; the resulting wine will be better for it.

If the malolactic fermentation of Chardonnay wine does not occur spontaneously, you can take a small quantity of red wine in which malaolactic fermentation is taking place, and add it to the the secondary fermentor, or carboy, which contains the Chardonnay, to induce fermentation. The addition of 100 ml. (3 fl. oz.) of red wine will not affect the colour of your Chardonnay. As an alternative to the above method, malolactic bacteria for the same purpose are available from your retailer.

As for other white musts, proceed in the same manner as for red, leaving out the malolactic fermentation stage.

Throughout the entire winemaking process, remember to log your essential data (density readings, tastings, etc.) on your record card.

- Allow a primary fermentation of 5 -7 days (it may take up to 10 days).
- Verify the density by taking a specific gravity reading with the hydrometer (remember to disinfect the hydro-

meter and its cylinder by sulphiting them and rinsing them well with purified water before every reading; rinse them after use as well). Note the S.G. readings on your winemaking record card throughout the process, for reference purposes. If the reading is 1.020 or less, siphon the wine into a 20- or 23-litre secondary fermentor (carboy).

- After 21 days, verify if fermentation has finished: the specific gravity reading should now be 0.995 or less for dry wines, and 0.998 for sweeter wines.

From this point onward, the procedures for making wine from fresh white musts differ slightly from those for red musts.

- Siphon the must into another carboy, adding one level quarter-teaspoon of potassium metabisulphite to prevent malolactic fermentation from occurring.
- Allow the wine to age in the carboy(s) for 3 - 9 months. A low temperature is perfectly all right for white wines; if your carboys are in the basement, there is no need to fit them with heating belts, or to heat the room.
- To complete the vinification of the white must, proceed in the same manner as for red must, that is, add a quarter-teaspoon of potassium metabisulphite three days before adding the stabilizer, the clarifiers and the optional products (oak chips, sweetener, etc.), and filter the wine before bottling.

Fresh refrigerated must requires more time to mature than sterilized or concentrated must. It is strongly recommended to wait one year after the beginning of fermentation before drinking the wine. Thus, it should be allowed to age in the bottle at least three months.

The shortest waiting period before drinking wine made from fresh must is six months (including three months in the bottle), but this is really not recommended, as the wine will still be far from reaching its optimum maturity.

Primary Fermentation

- Allow the temperature of the must to reach at least 20°C (68°F).
- Siphon or pour into the primary fermentor.
- Take an initial S.G. (density) reading.
- Add yeast if necessary.
- Cover with lid or plastic sheeting.
- Let ferment at a stable temperature between 20°C - 30°C (68°F - 86°F).

Day 0 - 6

Secondary Fermentation

- At an S.G. reading of 1.020, rack into a secondary fermentor.
- Install the fermentation lock and pour standard metabisulphite solution into it.
- On the 21st day, rack.
- Proceed with malolactic fermentation.

Day 7 to 21

Bulk Aging, or *Cuvaison*

- Let stand 2 or 3 months.
- At an S.G. reading of 0.995 (dry wines) or 0.998 (sweeter wines), fermentation is finished.
- Add potassium metabisulphite.
- Three days later, add stabilizer, clarifiers, metatartric crytstals, and other (optional) additives (oak chips, sweeteners, etc.).

Day 22 to 112
(3 months)

Maturation

- One month later, filter your wine.
- Bottle and age for at least 3 months, taking measures to prevent refermentation after bottling.
- Allow to age at least 1 year (in total) in carboys or bottles before drinking.

Day 113 to 142
(1 month)

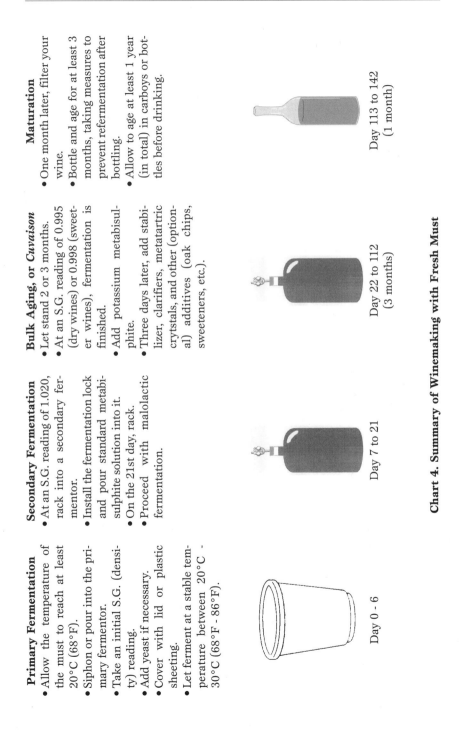

Chart 4. Summary of Winemaking with Fresh Must

Making Wine from Whole Grapes

As we suggested in Chapter 5, making wine with whole grapes should only be undertaken after a few years' experience. Firstly, because the operation is longer and more complicated, and secondly, because there is a greater risk of failure than when working with fresh and sterilized musts or concentrates, which are almost always already balanced.

Another danger with whole grapes bought in bulk from wholesalers is that they may be contaminated by rot or bacteria.

Thus warned, if you are still determined to make your own wine from scratch, it is safer to follow the steps recommended here rather than those suggested by the grape-sellers, or you may end up with a crude, semi-sparkling wine from a recipe that hasn't been adapted to the new and better methods that are now used in home winemaking.

Only a connoisseur can be sure of buying the right grapes for making wine. It is not a rare occurrence for amateur winemakers to make mistakes, believing that they are buying a noble variety of grapes, whereas this may not be the case at all. The name on the box doesn't guarantee that the grapes inside it actually belong to that variety!

In any case, you should choose fully ripened grapes. This is an important detail, especially because grapes are often picked underripe to prevent them from spoiling before they reach the stores or the market. Some years, the grapes will contain less than the ideal amount of sugar. In that case, you will have to make adjustments to the must, or the final result will necessarily be inferior. Watch out for mould: if there is a lot of it, don't buy the grapes.

Vinification Method for Whole Grapes (Red Wine)

It is especially important to always note down all your data (density readings, tastings, malolactic activity, etc.) on your winemaking record card throughout the following process.

- Buy a minimum of two 16-kilogram (36-lb.) cases of red grapes (called "lugs") to make 20 litres of wine (each case will produce about 10 litres).
- Destem the grapes to prevent the stalks and stems from being crushed with the grapes, which would produce an excess of tannin. The grape-crushers now available to home winemakers include a destemming mechanism which eliminates the necessity of doing this by hand.
- Crush the grapes. The teeth of the crushing apparatus perforates and tears the grapeskins, allowing the grapes to release all of their juice.
- If, during this operation, you discover that there is more mould or rot than you had noticed when buying the grapes, add one level quarter-teaspoon of potassium metabisulphite crystals dissolved in 60 ml. (2 fl. oz.) of lukewarm water to the amount of must made from two cases of grapes. This additive may, however, slow down or arrest the malolactic fermentation stage, which may have to be reactivated later on.
- Take an initial density reading of a sample of the must, passed through a plastic strainer, or sieve (if the must isn't sieved, this operation will be difficult), using the hydrometer. Remember to always sanitize and rinse the hydrometer and its cylinder every time you use them, and note down the readings for reference purposes. If the density is too low, that is, if the specific gravity is less than 1.080, add one cup of dextrose (or sugar) per 20- or 23-litre quantity, which should increase the density by .005. If, on the other hand, the initial specific

gravity is too high, that is, above 1.100, add 2 cups of water per 20 or 23 litres of must.

- Using the appropriate testing apparatus, take a reading of the total acid content and balance the must (see Chapters 3 and 7). The ideal acidity rate is between 5 and 6 grams per litre (g/l) for red wine, and between 5 and 7 g/l for white wines. Note that the acidity rate of must made from whole grapes tends to lose one gram per litre (1.0 g/l) during fermentation; therefore, it is better to start with a higher level than with a lower one. If you possess a pH-meter, take a pH reading of the must: the pH level should be between 3.1 and 3.5; the ideal level is 3.3.

- Add the yeast to the must. You should choose the type of yeast that is appropriate to your needs. You may opt for yeast which encourages malolactic fermentation (the D47-type), or K1V-1116-type yeasts when there is mould on the grapes. Follow the directions on the packet to prepare the yeast, then inoculate the must with it.

- Cover the primary fermentor, either with its own lid, or with plastic sheeting held down around the rim with a string or cord tied to elastic bands, or one giant-sized elastic band.

- Let stand to ferment in a warm place protected from draughts (at a temperature between 20°C and 30°C, or 68°F and 86°F); if the area is too cold, place a heating belt (available at winemaking shops) around the fermentor. In the case of red wine, when malolactic fermentation is desired, this temperature (20°C - 30°C, or 68°F - 86°F) must be maintained for three months. A heating belt is almost certainly required if the must is fermented in an unheated basement.

- "Punch down" the cap (the layer of grape residue that forms on the surface of the must) at least twice and up to four times every day. This operation is done for three reasons: first, to mix the skins, seeds, and other residue with the must to impart colour and tannins; second, to release the accumulated heat created by the ferment, which, if held captive under the cap, can go over 35°C (94°F), at which point fermentation may suddenly stop; third, if the cap is left on the surface for a period between 24 and 30 hours, mould can form and spoil the wine. If the fermenting must does overheat, cool it down with cold water or ice (this can be done by holding a sterilized, sealed bag of ice inside the must), then fermentation will most likely resume.

- To obtain the desired colour and the appropriate amount of tannin, the must should be left with its skins for a period varying between three and seven days. The skins can be removed from the must irrespective of its density; it is not necessary to wait until the primary fermentation process is over before doing this.

- Siphon as much of the must as possible into the secondary fermentor, or carboy, that has been washed, disinfected, and rinsed with purified water. Put the grape residue into a wine press. This is a cylindrical container inside which the residue is pressed downward by a lid activated by a large vertical screw turned slowly by a rotary handle. The press is composed of spaced wooden lathes (see Chapter 4) and is a rather expensive piece of equipment. Press the residue, but not too much: it should not become a hard compact mass. Verify the quality of the juice being pressed out: if it is becoming bitter, stop pressing the residue and add only the juice already obtained to the rest of the must.

- Fill the secondary fermentor, leaving 5 cm. (2 in.) between the surface of the wine and the bottom of the stopper or bung, unless the ferment is still too active (that is, if the surface is still frothing). If this is the case, to prevent the must from overflowing, leave a leeway of 10 cm. (4 in.), and top up the wine (leaving the 5-cm. or 2-in. leeway) one or two days later with more wine (preferably from the same batch); it is not recommanded not to use water in this case.

- We strongly recommend that you use glass carboys when making wine from whole grapes. In this method, the wine will remain in the carboy for more than three months, which leaves enough time for oxygen to penetrate the must if plastic containers are used. If you have too much wine to go into the carboy(s), you can keep it in bottles, gallon jugs, or other recipients that can accomodate a fermentation lock.
- Install the fermentation lock and pour standard metabisulphite solution[20] into it to the indicated level. Cover the lock with its cap to protect it from dust and to slow evaporation inside it.

Bulk Aging, or Cuvaison

- On the 21st day after it began, fermentation should be finished (although this can take up to a month). Take a density reading: it should now be 0.995 (for dry wines) or 0.998 (for sweeter wines). Don't forget to sulphite and rinse the hydrometer and its cylinder every time you take a S.G. reading. Also, log the readings on your winemaking record card for reference purposes.
- If the density is still too high, prolong the fermentation process until the required specific gravity reading is obtained. This may necessitate putting the carboy in a warmer place to activate the process. If there is no activity, consult your winemaking equipment retailer to determine whether you should use restarter[21].

---

20. "Standard metabisulphite solution" means 50g. (9 level, not heaping, teaspoons) of potassium metabisulphite crystals dissolved in 4 litres (about a gallon) of lukewarm water.

- Carry out a taste trial. If the wine has a hydrogen sulphide, or rotten egg odour, you should immediately take measures to remedy the situation: add one level quarter-teaspoon of dissolved potassium metabisulphite crystals. Then siphon the wine three or four times into sanitized recipients to aerate it and to eliminate the sulphur odour.
- Rack the wine. If you do not have a second carboy, you can use the (sanitized) primary fermentor to hold the wine while you thoroughly clean the carboy. Siphon the wine back into it quickly to prevent too much air contact.
- Put the fermentation lock on the carboy; add standard metabisulphite solution to the appropriate level and cap the lock.
- Leave in the carboy for two or three months at a stable temperature (between 20°C and 30°C, or 68°F and 86°F).
- Verify whether malolactic fermentation has begun. If it has, you should see little bubbles rising continuously, and there will be visible activity inside the fermentation lock.
- If you are using several carboys and only some of them show malolactic fermentation activity, extract 100 ml. (3 fl. oz.) of must from a carboy in which there is ferment, and pour it into the carboys in which there is no perceptible action, to induce fermentation in them.
- Rack, according to the usual method, every four or six weeks if there is quite a lot of sediment in your wine.
- After two months, take a density reading, and verify the wine's taste, smell, and clarity to make sure everything is going well. If the malolactic fermentation stage has not taken place, the wine should be kept in the carboy(s) for another month, and it may be necessary to

21. For the preparation of restarter, see the beginning of this chapter (page 125).

use malolactic bacteria (bought from your retailer) to induce that fermentation stage.

- When the malolactic fermentation is over, there will be no more activity inside the fermentation lock. Add one quarter-teaspoon of metabisulphite crystals dissolved in lukewarm water to each 20- or 23-litre carboy.

- You may now add oak chips if you want your wine to have an oak cask flavour. The chips must first be sterilized: heat them in the oven for twenty minutes at a temperature of 90°C - 100°C (194°F - 212°F), but no hotter than that or they may acquire a burnt taste. Secure them in a cleesecloth or nylon net bag with a couple of sterilized glass marbles to hold them down at the bottom of the carboy. Oak flavour essence, on the other hand, can be added just before the filtration process.

- At this point, you must choose either to age your wine in the carboy(s) for a period of nine months starting from the first day of fermentation (and thus avoid the temptation of drinking the wine too young!), or to proceed with bottling immediately, by following the steps outlined below.

The following optional procedures should be carried out in the order in which they are described below:

- Add metatartric acid if you dislike the presence of those harmless tartrate deposits in wine after it is bottled. Another method is to make the crystals form before bottling, thus enabling you to remove them easily: keep the carboy at a low temperature (0°C or 32°F) for two or three weeks. Some winemakers leave their carboys outside in the cold for this purpose (but be careful that the wine doesn't freeze hard!). This solution also incurs greater risk to the wine because it implies additional handling; it would be safer to use an extra refrigerator, if you have one.

- Stabilize your wine with 2 teaspoons of potassium sorbate diluted in $^1/_4$ cup of purified water, for each 20 or

23 litres of wine. When wine has undergone malolactic fermentation, potassium sorbate stabilizer cannot be added unless the wine has been sterilized with a quarter-teaspoon of potassium metabisulphite (for 20 or 23 litres of wine) three days beforehand. This can be done easily by dissolving a quarter-teaspoon of meta crystals in 50 ml. ($1^2/3$ fl. oz.) of lukewarm water and stirring it vigorously into the wine. Note that if there is sediment at this time, racking should be done.

Treating the wine with metabisulphite three days before stabilizing it is a proven and effective method which almost infallibly prevents your wine from acquiring a geranium odour and becoming undrinkable. The stabilizer prevents the unwanted reoccurrence of fermentation once the wine has been bottled, which would lead to effervescence in the wine, or loss because of the corks shooting out of the bottles.

- When stabilizing has been done, clear the wine with isinglass fining, or with bentonite if the wine is cloudy. This operation is optional if you are planning to filter the wine.
- Add sweeteners if you like (to taste).

Bottling and Aging

- One month later, the wine can be filtered. If you do not own filtering equipment, it can be rented from a wine-making equipment store. This operation means a little additional time and effort, but the results are worth it: the wine becomes crystal-clear with an excellent consistency for drinking. Moreover, filtration prevents the lees (dead yeast-cell sediment) from giving the wine a bad taste when it has aged for several months.

- Bottle the wine; if you do not own a corking machine, you can rent this useful piece of equipment. Allow the bottles to stand upright for ten days.
- Drink your red wine one year after the beginning of fermentation, or even later. Home-made wine that is made from whole grapes generally has more body than wine made from concentrates or other forms of prepared must. It also improves with aging.

Vinification Method for Whole Grapes (White Wine)

Making white wine from whole grapes is not much different from the procedure for red wine. The two major differences are that pigmenting is not required, and the malolactic fermentation stage should not be allowed to take place when making white wine (except in the case of Chardonnay).

Thus, the steps are very similar in the two cases, with the notable exception that only the juice is kept and put to ferment immediately in the primary fermentor. As there is no grape residue, there will be no cap to lower or punch down every day during the first fermentation stage.

Also, the temperature does not have to be maintained between 20°C and 30°C (68°F - 86°F) for three months, as this encourages malolactic fermentation, which is not desirable when making white wine. The wine is better left at cool temperatures, that is, at around 18°C (62° or 63°F). One level quarter-teaspoon of metabisulphite crystals (per 20 or 23 litres of must) dissolved in water should be added during crushing and pressing (for sanitizing purposes) and again during the first racking, to halt the activity of the malolactic bacteria. The same amount of meta is added again at bottling time, in the same manner as for the red wine, that is, three days before adding the stabilizer.

Of course, some people like very dry wine, whereas others prefer it a little sweeter. If, at the time of bottling (but before

N.B.: Follow the appropriate steps for crushing and pressing the grapes, as well as for balancing the acids.

Primary Fermentation
- Take an initial S.G. (density) reading.
- Add the yeast.
- Cover with lid or plastic sheeting.
- Ferment at a temperature of 20-30°C (68-86°F) and punch down the cap 2 to 4 times every day.

Secondary Fermentation
- At a S.G. reading of 1.020, rack into a secondary fermentor.
- Press the grape residue and add juice to must.
- Install the fermentation lock and pour standard metabisulphite solution into it.
- On the 21st day, rack.
- Proceed with malolactic fermentation.

Bulk Aging, or *Cuvaison*
- Let stand 2 or 3 months.
- At a S.G. reading of 0.995 (dry wine) or 0.998 (sweet wine), fermentation is finished.
- Rack every month if sediment or lees subsist.
- Add sweeteners (optional).

Maturation
- One month later, filter your wine.
- Bottle and age for at least 3 months, taking measures to prevent refermentation after bottling.
- Allow to age at least 1 year (in total) in carboys or bottles before drinking.

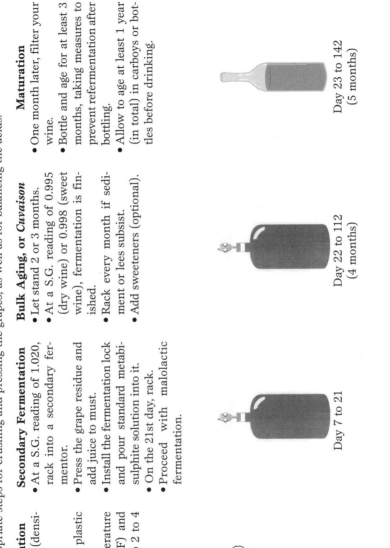

Day 0 - 6   Day 7 to 21   Day 22 to 112 (4 months)   Day 23 to 142 (5 months)

Chart 5. Summary of Winemaking with Whole Grapes

filtering), you find that your white wine is too dry, you can add CC (a product made by Tecvin, composed of 100 % pure grape sugar), or another type of sweetener which will make your wine a little less dry.

As for the rest of the procedure, the same steps are followed. White wine can be consumed earlier than red, as it is lower in tannin. However, it is always better to wait one year before drinking your wine, particularly when you are starting with whole grapes.

> *Must made directly from whole grapes requires more time to mature than sterilized or concentrated must. It is strongly recommended to wait one year after the beginning of fermentation before drinking the wine. Thus, it should be allowed to age in the bottle at least three months.*
>
> *The shortest waiting period before drinking wine made from fresh must is six months (including three months in the bottle), but this is really not recommended, as the wine will still be far from reaching its optimum maturity.*

How To Make Sparkling Wine

There are at least four methods for producing home-made sparkling wine. Whichever method is used, we first recommend that you pay careful attention when choosing the must, to make sure that it is appropriate for this purpose. For sparkling wines, either fresh or sterilized musts are the best. A less appropriate, but still feasible choice would be a semi-concentrate. We also recommend that you procure a must made from a classic grape variety; Chardonnay produces the best results. Moselle, Riesling and Gewürztraminer, as well as Muscat grapes, all make good sparkling wines. It is better to choose a must with a fairly strong taste, as the additional carbon dioxide gas masks the aroma of the wine somewhat, as well as making it dryer. Thus, it is preferable to start by making a wine with a well-defined aroma.

All sparkling wines should be drunk very cold, almost at freezing point. Note also that there is no sense in aging sparkling wine, as the carbon dioxide gas halts its natural maturation process.

The Closed Fermentor and Carbonation

The first and simplest method of making sparkling wine is that of the closed fermentor. Follow the procedures for making wine from fresh refrigerated or sterilized musts, not forgetting to stabilize it, until the bottling stage. This is when still wine can be transformed into sparkling wine. First, however, it is strongly recommended to get rid of any tartric crystals (this is optional in the case of still wines) by adding metatartric acid or by refrigerating the wine, as explained earlier in this chapter. The wine should also be filtered.

To accomplish the transformation of still wine into sparkling wine, a 19-litre stainless steel container or tank is required. These are available at some winemaking shops. Most of them previously served as pressure tanks to hold soft drinks; thus, they are able to withstand strong internal pressure.

When the wine is ready for bottling, siphon it into the stainless steel container. It can now be sweetened (only in this method, not in the other three), using certain speciality products obtainable at winemaking supply stores: CC, made by Tecvin (100 % natural grape sugar), Dolce, or wine conditioner. You can also reserve a little of the must before fermenting and add it as a sweetener when the wine is bottled. We suggest that you add only 125 ml.

Dolce and CC,
wine sweeteners.

(^{1}/2 cup) of sweetener or unfermented must to 19 litres of fermented must. For very sweet sparkling wine, however, you can add up to 250 ml. (one cup) of sweetener or unfermented must.

Regulate the carbon dioxide pressure to 3.26 kg/cm^2 (45 lb. per sq. in.). The container is then placed inside a refrigerator at a temperature near 0°C (32°F) for one week, while maintaining the pressure at the same level throughout.

To bottle sparkling wine, a special apparatus is needed; it can be rented. For this operation to be successful, the bottles themselves must be very cold. Only bottles made expressly to hold sparkling wines can be used: ordinary bottles can explode after some time, which may cause serious injury. Immediately after filling the bottle, the stopper must be inserted and well-secured with Champagne wire to prevent it from shooting out. Metal capsules over the stopper and neck will give a more festive, elegant air to your bottle of sparkling wine. The additional cost of the above operations amounts to about $1 per bottle.

The results are surprisingly good, especially if the sparkling wine is left to age for at least one month. The carbon dioxide then has time to fully integrate the wine, and it will bubble longer when it is served in a glass.

Most people who have used this method to produce sparkling wine enjoy it, and many of them now carry out the operation once or even several times a year!

The Closed Fermentor and Refermentation

The second method of making sparkling wine is to induce refermentation in a sealed fermentor. As in the preceding method, the operation is only done after the wine is clear and ready for bottling (this time period varies according to the type of must used). The base wine should not have an alcohol content higher than 11.5 % (23° Proof).

Warning: the wine should not be stabilized in this method, as refermentation is to be induced by adding yeast and sugar. The EC-1118 Champagne-type yeast should be used, as it is the most resistant to the alcohol already contained in the wine.

This method is similar to the previous one in that the wine is siphoned into a stainless steel container and sugar is added to allow carbon dioxide gas to form inside the container. You can use either one cup of sugar for 19 litres of wine, or 1 $^1/_4$ cup of dextrose. We recommend using the dextrose, as it encourages fermentation better.

When this operation is finished, add restarter made from EC-1118-type yeast. Stir, and dissolve the yeast thoroughly. Close the container tightly, and allow the wine to referment, keeping it at a temperature of 16°C - 20°C (60°F - 70°F) for 4 - 6 weeks.

Bottle (in sparkling wine bottles only) in the same manner as in the carbonation method.

Note that the first bottle of sparkling wine obtained by this method will inevitably be cloudy. When siphoning begins, the end of the tube will suck up any existing residue from the bottom of the container. The subsequent bottles of wine will be clear.

This method is more complex than the first one, and the results are not remarkably better.

Some people find that adding carbon dioxide gas is easier, while others view the refermentation of the wine as a more natural method. It's simply a matter of personal inclination, as there is not much difference in the results. However, if you opt for the second method, you should realize that the stainless steel container has to stand for at least a month, and consequently, you will most likely have to buy your own container, instead of renting or borrowing one.

The Méthode champenoise

In the *méthode champenoise* (the word *Champagne* only applies to winemaking activity carried out in the actual Champagne region, using particular blending procedures), the basic rules are the same as in the two preceding methods. The wine must be ready for maturing; in the *méthode champenoise*, the base wine should not have an alcohol content higher than 11.5 % (23° Proof). To encourage refermentation in the bottles, no stabilizer should be used. Add metatartric acid, or refrigerate the must to facilitate the elimination of tartrate deposits before bottling. If the

A bottle of sparkling wine.

wine is not perfectly clear, filter. Then stir either one cup of sugar or 1 $^1/_4$ cup of dextrose into each 20 litres of wine. Stir in restarter made with EC-1118-type yeast.

The next step is bottling, using bottles made for sparkling wines only. In the *méthode champenoise*, you have to use caps made for beer bottles, and a capper[22]. When all the bottles are capped, let them stand for 6 - 12 weeks at a temperature of 15°C - 20°C (60°F - 70°F). Then, remove the cap of one bottle to verify if enough gas is present; if so, proceed with disgorging.

Disgorging is a delicate operation, done after all the yeast sediment formed during the refermentation process has gradually settled in the neck of the bottle. This is achieved by placing the bottles upside-down in cardboard cartons, and giving each bottle a half-turn every day during two or three weeks. Winemakers with money to spend can buy a *pupitre*, or clearing rack, and tilt the bottles a little more every two or three days until they are completely upside-down.

Thus, when all the sediment is lodged in the neck, against the stopper, it is time for disgorging. Unless you are a past master at this skill, we do not recommend that you carry it out at room temperature, or you may lose two-thirds of your production, and probably your patience as well. Our suggestion is to freeze part of the sparkling wine so that you can extract only the small frozen portion next to the stopper.

There are two ways to do this. The first is to prepare a brine, by mixing one part of coarse salt with 4 parts of crushed ice, in a large tub. The bottles are stuck upside-down in the ice and salt, deep enough so that the contents will be allowed to freeze up to a level of about 1.25 cm. ($^1/_2$ in.) above the sediment layer in the neck.

When this level has frozen, you can begin disgorging. Speed is of the essence in this operation if you want to keep

---

22. Be careful what type of bottle you are using: in Europe, caps are made according to metric measurements and are slightly bigger than the caps made in North America. The bottles, the caps, and the capper must all be compatible.

most of your sparkling wine. Place an empty recipient (the primary fermentor will do) on a slant in front of you (between your legs, or propped against something solid) and remove the cap of the bottle. Hold the frozen part of the neck firmly, pointing it towards the pail (or other recipient) and wait until the pressure expels the frozen sediment into the recipient (with any luck). Then, stop up the neck immediately with your thumb. After about fifteen seconds, take a sterilized plastic stopper with your free hand and forcefully insert it into the neck of the bottle.

Tie down the cap with a wire hood (Champagne wire) so that it cannot shoot out. Repeat this procedure with each of the bottles.

It takes considerable dexterity to accomplish the disgorging of sparkling wine without waste or mess. This is why we suggest that the amateur winemaker try it first with dummy bottles to acquire some practice in doing it. At the same time as you are adding the sugar and yeast to referment your wine, fill a certain number of bottles (6 - 10) with water and add to each bottle the juice of half a lemon, one level teaspoon of dextrose, and some EC-1118-type yeast. This mixture will become bubbly at the same time as the wine does; thus, you will be able to make several trial runs (don't forget that this is a dangerous sport!) to gain the necessary skill for disgorging your sparkling wine.

As you can imagine, this method is far from easy, especially if you are doing it alone. It requires concentration, exceptional dexterity, and a strong thumb, if success is to be attained with any certainty. It is not really recommended for amateur winemakers, unless they are resolutely determined, as there is a very high probability of losing a large part of the product.

The Méthode champenoise *Made Easy*

Making sparkling wine by the *méthode champenoise* is not difficult in itself; it is only the disgorging procedure that has intimidated many a good winemaker. Aware of this difficulty, the manufacturers of winemaking accessories have invented special stoppers which allow the sediment to be sealed off, or expelled through the stopper itself.

There are several different models available. The first is a 10 cm. (4 in.) stopper made so that the yeast sediment will collect inside its cylinder. When all the sediment is contained in the cylinder, the flexible part of it can simply be folded over and attached.

Another model has a little valve in it, that can be opened by pulling a string at the appropriate moment, allowing the sediment to spew out of the bottle before it is shut again.

Both of these little accessories are quite ingenious... in principle. However, they do not provide the total control that one might hope for. Some of these special stoppers are not completely air-tight, and you may lose a certain number of bottles of sparkling wine if the gas escapes. This defect will most likely be rectified in the near future, but in the meantime, the rate of loss is too significant (between 20 % and 25 %) for us to recommend them unconditionally.

Problems and their Solutions

The winemaking process is relatively easy to carry out. Generally speaking, success is not difficult to attain. However certain problems may arise, and it is better to be forewarned, so that you will know how to deal with them.

To end this chapter on winemaking procedures, we have included some of the more common problems that you might face while making your own wine, together with our suggested solutions to them.

> *One very important recommendation that applies to the entire process is that you always use lukewarm water for dissolving or diluting the products to be added to the must or to the wine. This technique, known as hydrolization, prevents a too-violent reaction when a chemical property comes into direct contact with the must.*

Sluggish Fermentation

It happens quite often that the amateur winemaker notices that fermentation has barely progressed even after about ten days. The hydrometer registers a specific gravity of 1.040 instead of the desired reading of 1.020.

In many cases, sluggishness in fermentation occurs when the temperature of the must is decidedly too low to allow normal fermentation.

If this is the cause, the solution is simple: raise the temperature of the must, either by placing a heating belt around the outside of the fermentor, or by raising the room temperature. At the same time, to help reactivate the fermentation process, we suggest occasionally stirring the must gently with a long plastic spoon (available at winemaking supply stores) during the first three or four days that fermentation is being reactivated. Don't forget to sanitize the utensil before use.

Fermentation Will Not Start

Occasionally, the fermentation process will not get off the ground. This is usually due to insufficient warmth (see above), but if warming the must doesn't help, the problem might lie in the preparation of the yeast. The directions on the packet must always be followed very carefully. The water used must not be too hot. Do not leave the yeast mixture too long before adding it to the must: yeast cells multiply very rapidly, and they need room, food, and vitamins to survive and proliferate. If they only have water, the yeast cells will starve and die.

To start fermentation, you will have to make a new yeast mixture to add to the must. Mixing yeast into your must several times will not harm it. The more yeast there is, the more likely it is that the fermentation process will get going again.

Another possible reason that fermentation will not start is that the total sulphur dioxide rate may be too high. In this specific case, you must prepare restarter [23].

Stuck Fermentation

It sometimes happens that fermentation suddenly stops. This occurs when the specific gravity of the must is between 1.010 and 1.020, and is often due to an excess of carbon dioxide and a lack of oxygen, a combination which halts yeast activity. Aerating by "spread-out" racking will give the must the oxygen it needs.

---

23. The preparation of restarter is explained at the beginning of this chapter (page 125).

This situation may also be the result of a low temperature, in which case, the temperature should be raised. Another reason may be an overly high alcohol content, which causes the yeast cells to die. This is why it is important to take a density reading of the must before the beginning of the winemaking process: if the specific gravity is more than 1.100, it means that there is too much sugar in the must. To correct this situation, we suggest adding pure spring water or distilled water in a proportion not exceeding 5 % of the total volume of the must, that is, one litre of water for 20 litres of must.

If none of these suggested measures have any effect, other means must be used. It serves no purpose to add more yeast if the density reading is already too low (1.010 - 1.020). Fresh yeast cannot acclimatize to such a high alcohol rate, and will not be able to survive. You will have to prepare restarter, according to the method explained at the beginning of this chapter (page 125), taking care to lower the density until it corresponds to the density at which the must had stopped fermenting.

Rotten Egg, or Sulphur Odour

The reasons that bring about this sulphurous, or rotten egg smell are too diverse and complicated to describe here. Immediate action is necessary to get rid of this odour, and at the same time, to save the must from being irreparably spoiled. Add one level quarter-teaspoon of potassium metabisulphite and one teaspoon of Vitamin C (ascorbic acid), dissolved in 60 ml. (¹/₄ cup) of spring water or distilled water, to every 20 or 23 litres of must, then carry out three or four "spread-out" rackings in succession. If this doesn't solve the problem, then you can try a rather rough-and-ready chemical treatment, that is, pour the must through a copper funnel or add copper sulphate to it. If you have written down the lot number of your must and have told your retailer about the problem, you may be able to have your guarantee honoured, depending on the

integrity or customer relations policy of the company that distributes the must.

Oxidized Sulphur Odour

When the must gives off a smell reminiscent of a wooden
match being lit, it is probably because too much potassium
metabisulphite has been used. To know for sure, you can subject the must to a metabisulphite test, using a titration kit
made by the CHEMetrics company, usually available at winemaking speciality shops. This test is described in detail in
Chapter 7. The only way to solve this problem is to gradually
allow the gas generated by the oxidation of the sulphur to
escape via the fermentation lock, or to carry out one or two
"spread-out" rackings, that is, siphon the wine so that it speads
over the inside walls of the carboy, giving it a chance to aerate.
Above all, do not bottle your wine unless this odour has gone.

Geranium Odour

This phenomenon occurs mainly when making wine
from fresh refrigerated must, or from whole grapes that you
have crushed and pressed yourself, and the proper procedure
for stabilizing the wine has not been carried out. As we mentioned earlier, it is essential that one level quarter-teaspoon of
potassium metabisulphite (dissolved in lukewarm water) be
added three days before dissolving the potassium sorbate in the
wine. The unpleasant geranium smell is the result of neglect-
ing this important detail.

*Unfortunately, if you have neglected to follow the proper pro-
cedure in stabilizing your wine, and this tell-tale odour man-
ifests itself, you will have to face the fact that your wine is
spoiled.*

Overly Acidic Wine

If you find that your wine is too acidic (if it tastes bitter), carry out an acidity test (see Chapters 3 and 7 for details), and if necessary, lower the acidity rate with an acid-lowering product, available in winemaking supply stores. It should be added little by little every few days, testing and tasting every time until the desired acidity rate is achieved.

Colour Problems

Red wines may occasionally be too pale for your taste. This often happens if the pigmentation process was too short[24]. You can correct a weakness in colour with powdered or liquid colouring agents, available from your supplier. But don't go overboard: a Cabernet Sauvignon wine shouldn't be dark red! If you are particular about colour, you can compare your product with the *appellation contrôlée* wines at the liquor store. In this area, as you might imagine, moderation is the best policy.

On the other hand, if your white wine has a caramel hue, or worse, a brownish tinge, it is possible to clear the colour, but this should only be done on condition that the wine is drinkable, that is, if it has not discoloured as a result of oxidation. In any case, take a sample to show your winemaking specialist: if the wine is considered good, you will be able to give it a more pleasing colour by using an activated carbon filter, or powder. This technique generally restores the white wine's desired colour.

---

24. See Chapters 1 and 2 for more information about pigmenting.

Measurements, Scales and Tests

We have included all the measurement equivalents and conversion tables that you might need in this one comprehensive chapter. It also contains information and explanations about the different tests that are current in home winemaking. Thus, this chapter serves as an easily accessible reference source that you can consult throughout the winemaking process if you need to verify any of its technical aspects.

Some of the tests are somewhat complicated to perform, while others are very simple. Although we realize that many home winemakers may not carry out all of these tests, we have included the full range of tests, scientific explanations, and technical data for the benefit of those who might require it.

Measurement Equivalents

SMALL LIQUID VOLUMES	
Metric	**Imperial**
45 ml.	3 tablespoons
30 ml.	2 tablespoons
15 ml.	1 tablespoon
5 ml.	1 teaspoon
2.5 ml.	1/2 teaspoon
1.25 ml.	1/4 teaspoon

Temperature Equivalents

Degrees Celsius	Degrees Fahrenheit
100	212.0
90	194.0
80	176.0
70	158.0
60	140.0
50	122.0
40	104.0
30	86.0
29	84.2
28	82.4
27	80.6
26	78.8
25	77.0
24	75.2
23	73.4
22	71.6
21	69.8
20	68.0
19	66.2
18	64.4
17	62.6
16	60.8
15	59.0
10	50.0
5	41.0
0	32.0

Larger Liquid Volumes

LIQUID VOLUMES ($^1/_2$ - 1 LITRE)		
Metric	**Imperial**	
1.0 litre	4 cups	32 fluid oz.
500.0 ml.	2 cups	16 fluid oz.
437.5 ml.	1 $^3/_4$ cups	14 fluid oz.
416.5 ml.	1 $^2/_3$ cups	13 $^1/_3$ fluid oz.
375.0 ml.	1 $^1/_2$ cups	12 fluid oz.
333.3 ml.	1 $^1/_3$ cups	10 $^2/_3$ fluid oz.
312.5 ml.	1 $^1/_4$ cups	10 fluid oz.
250.0 ml.	1 cup	8 fluid oz.
187.5 ml.	$^3/_4$ cup	6 fluid oz.
165.0 ml.	$^2/_3$ cup	5 $^2/_7$ fluid oz.
125.0 ml.	$^1/_2$ cup	4 fluid oz.
82.5 ml.	$^1/_3$ cup	2 $^2/_3$ fluid oz.
62.5 ml.	$^1/_4$ cup	2 fluid oz.

DEMI-JOHNS AND CARBOYS					
100	litres (l.)	22	Imp. gal.	26	U.S. gal.
54	litres	12	Imp. gal.	14	U.S. gal.
30	litres	6.6	Imp. gal.	7.9	U.S. gal.
28	litres	6.1	Imp. gal.	7.4	U.S. gal.
23	litres	5.1	Imp. gal.	6.1	U.S. gal.
20	litres	4.4	Imp. gal.	5.3	U.S. gal.
19	litres	4.2	Imp. gal.	5	U.S. gal.
18	litres	4	Imp. gal.	4.75	U.S. gal.
15	litres	3.25	Imp. gal.	4	U.S. gal.
11	litres	2.4	Imp. gal.	3	U.S. gal.
8	litres	1.8	Imp. gal.	2.1	U.S. gal.
4	litres	0.9	Imp. gal.	1	U.S. gal.

Dosage for Products Commonly Used in Winemaking

Potassium Metabisulphite (Sterilant)

- In powder form: one level quarter-teaspoon dissolved in lukewarm water is sufficient to sterilize 20 or 23 litres of must. The metabisulphite content is then 30 parts per million (ppm). Potassium metabisulphite is usually added three times during the winemaking process (therefore, 90 ppm in total). The established international standard for commercial wineries is a much higher 250 ppm.
- In tablet form: 3 tablets added 3 times (3 x 3) are sufficient for 20 or 23 litres of must.
- In standard solution (in a 4-litre/1 gal. container or in a vaporizer): metabisulphite solution is used for sterilizing fermentors, carboys, and bottles before use, and for sulphiting, or spraying, the instruments required during the winemaking process (eg. the hydrometer and its cylinder).
  Dissolve 9 level teaspoons or 3 level tablespoons (50 g.) of metabisulphite crystals in 4 litres of water (just under a gallon) to obtain a standard-strength disinfectant solution.

Warning: Glass recipients are strongly recommended. If plastic recipients are used (especially in the case of the vaporizer), the solution must be replaced after three months, before it loses its strength.

Warning: Use only potassium metabisulphite for this purpose. Sodium metabisulphite may be harmful to the health. Fortunately, it is rarely sold these days.

Warning: When making wine from fresh refrigerated red musts or Chardonnay must, do not add potassium metabisulphite between the primary and the secondary fermentation stages, as this would prevent the desired malolactic fermentation from occurring over the subsequent weeks.

Potassium Sorbate

Potassium sorbate is used to stabilize the wine just before filtering, to prevent refermentation in the bottle.

Warning: When making wine from fresh must, or from whole grapes, it is essential to add one level quarter-teaspoon of potassium metabisulphite dissolved in lukewarm water three days before *adding the potassium sorbate stabilizer.*

- Two teaspoons (6 g.) will stabilize 20 or 23 litres of wine.

Bentonite

- Three teaspoons are sufficient to clarify 20 or 23 litres of wine. The bentonite is mixed in one cup (250 ml.) of lukewarm, purified water. Complete dissolution does not occur; to achieve the best possible results, we suggest using a blender or a food processor. Pour in the water first, then add the bentonite in tiny doses while the blender or processor is on; this operation should take about two or three minutes to complete. For the bentonite to integrate better with the water, we suggest preparing the solution 24 hours before using it.

Isinglass

- Either one packet of powder (4 gm.), or one 25-ml. bottle, dissolved or diluted in lukewarm water, is sufficient to clarify 20 or 23 litres of wine.

Kielselsol, or Claro K.C.

- One packet of Kielselsol, or Claro K.C., will clarify 20 or 23 litres of wine. Follow the directions provided.

Oak Flavour Extract, or Essence

- For red wine: 50 ml. (1 $^3/_4$ fl. oz.) of oak flavour extract per 20 or 23 litres of wine.
- For white wine: 25 ml. ($^7/_8$ fl. oz.) of oak flavour extract per 20 or 23 litres of wine.

The quantities given above are only suggestions. If the wine has a very full body, more than the suggested amount can be added (75 ml., or 2$^1/_4$ fl. oz., for example). However, remember that moderation is the ideal when using flavour additives.

Oak Chips

- 30 grams (1 oz.) of oak chips, or moar (oak sawdust) are enough to instill the desired hint of oak-cask aging in the wine. The chips should be left in the wine from four to eight weeks, depending on the type of wine and the amount of flavour desired. Chips should not be left in white wine as long as in red.

Reading and Applying Hydrometer Measurements

The Hydrometer

The hydrometer is an instrument of prime importance in winemaking, required throughout the process. Therefore, it should be handled carefully to avoid breaking it (there is no point in having to spend money to replace your hydrometer two or three times a year!) and to avoid skewing the readings. The paper scale is only lightly glued inside the stem of the instrument, and rough or sloppy handling can dislodge it and falsify the readings.

From time to time, you should verify that the measurement paper is in place. If it stays fast inside the stem when you tilt, lightly shake, or turn the hydrometer upside-down, you can continue using the instrument. If the paper scale moves, or if you are not sure that it is in the right place, you should carry out a precision test (see below) before using it again.

Precision Test

The best way to carry out a precision test on your hydrometer is to fill its cylinder, or jar, with distilled water and lower the water temperature to 15°C (59°F) by refrigerating it for a few minutes. Take a density reading. If the temperature-corrected (see page 195) specific gravity reading is 1.000, then your hydrometer is properly calibrated. If, however, the reading is clearly above or below this benchmark, you will know that you can no longer trust your hydrometer to give you an accurate reading, and you'll have to buy a new one.

Reading the Hydrometer

Capillarity, or surface tension, is a phenomenon that occurs when liquids are contained inside tubes (as when the hydrometer is used): the liquid clings to the sides of the tube, thus creating the illusion that the level is higher than it actually is. The must or the wine will slope upwards where it comes into contact with the glass sides of both the hydrometer's stem and its cylinder, or jar. The resulting crescent is called the meniscus (see illustration). Thus, in hydrometer readings, there will obviously be a distortion in the indicator level on the inner surface of the cylinder as well as on the outer surface of the stem of the instrument itself. To avoid obtaining an inaccurate result, you must be careful to take the reading from the lowest point of the surface of the liquid (see illustration). If not, the reading may be off by one or even two degrees (for example, the S.G. reading would be 1.000 instead of 0.998, a significant difference in the vinification process). If you do take the reading at the top of the little

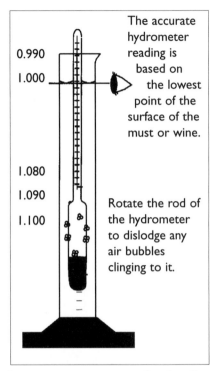

The accurate hydrometer reading is based on the lowest point of the surface of the must or wine.

Rotate the rod of the hydrometer to dislodge any air bubbles clinging to it.

curve, you'll have to adjust it in consequence to obtain the accurate S.G.

Air Bubbles

You should also make sure that there are no air bubbles present in the cylinder when you take your hydrometer readings; if these are allowed to remain, gross inaccuracies may occur. The bubbles tend to form in clusters around the bulbous part of the hydrometer. They will rise up when you rotate the hydrometer's stem gently.

Variations in the Readings

The S.G. scale of the hydrometer is established according to conditions prevailing at a particular temperature (15°C, or 59°F); thus, for maximum accuracy, you should take your readings when the must or the wine is at that temperature. It is probable that most of your winemaking activities are taking place at a room temperature somewhere between 15°C and 22°C (59°F and 71.6°F); however the variation in the readings caused by the higher temperature will be too slight to make any significant difference (probably not exceeding .5% - 1% of 1.000).

Thus, the variation table below is mainly for information purposes, unless you like your room temperature to be tropical. In that case, corrections will be needed when you use your hydrometer:

With a must/wine temp. of:	the variation will be:
10°C (50°F)	- 0.6
20°C (68°F)	+ 0.9
25°C (77°F)	+ 2.0
30°C (85°F)	+ 3.4
35°C (95°F)	+ 5.0
40°C (104°F)	+ 6.8

Alcohol Rates and the Hydrometer

There are three ways to determine the alcohol content of wine with a hydrometer.

The Potential Alcohol Scale

Many hydrometers include a scale called the Potential Alcohol (PA) scale. To know the alcohol content of your wine, you should take the PA reading at the same time as the density reading, that is, an initial reading when the must is about to start fermenting. At this point, a typical PA rate would be 11°. The next PA [1] reading is taken at the end of the last stage of fermentation (preferably just before bottling). If fermentation has been completely successful, the PA should be 0. To obtain the alcohol content, simply subtract the final PA reading from the initial reading, as in our example, 11° - 0° = 11°, or 11% alcohol. Another example: if the initial PA reading is 12°, and the final reading is 1°, the alcohol rate would be 12° - 1° = 11°, or 11% alcohol.

Calculating the Alcohol Rate from the Density Reading

You can calculate the alcoholic strength of your wine from the density, or specific gravity reading on your hydrometer. Always note down the initial density reading on your winemaking record card. At the end of fermentation (just before bottling is a good time), take a final density reading and subtract the final S.G. from the initial one. The result is divided by a number which is based on the initial density reading (see table opposite) to obtain the alcohol rate in the wine.

Let us give an example of how this formula works:

(a) Initial density (S.G.) reading: 1.085; (b) Final density (S.G.) reading: 0.990. We subtract (b) from (a): 1.085 - 0.990 = 0.095, or 95. We then divide this result by the appropriate divider (see table), that is: 95 ÷ 7.43 = 12.78%. The alcohol rate is therefore 12.8% per volume of wine (rounded figure).

---

1. The (U.S.) degree Proof simply corresponds to double the alcohol percent by volume. (see page 200 for examples).

Dividers (based on the initial density readings)

Initial Density	U.S. Divider Degrees Proof	Divider % alcohol/ volume	Initial Density	U.S. Divider Degrees Proof	Divider % alcohol/ volume
1.005	3.87	7.73	1.085	3.72	7.43
1.010	3.86	7.71	1.090	3.71	7.41
1.015	3.85	7.69	1.095	3.70	7.39
1.020	3.84	7.67	1.100	3.69	7.37
1.025	3.83	7.66	1.105	3.68	7.35
1.030	3.82	7.64	1.110	3.67	7.34
1.035	3.81	7.62	1.115	3.66	7.32
1.040	3.80	7.60	1.120	3.65	7.30
1.045	3.79	7.58	1.125	3.64	7.28
1.050	3.78	7.56	1.130	3.63	7.26
1.055	3.77	7.54	1.135	3.62	7.24
1.060	3.76	7.52	1.140	3.61	7.22
1.065	3.75	7.50	1.145	3.60	7.20
1.070	3.75	7.49	1.150	3.60	7.19
1.075	3.74	7.47	1.155	3.59	7.17
1.080	3.73	7.45	1.160	3.58	7.15

Determining the Alcohol Rate without Initial Density or PA Readings

The amateur winemaker may occasionally forget to write down the initial density reading, and is even more likely to forget to note the PA reading at the beginning of the vinification process. All is not lost: you can still enjoy your wine without knowing the exact alcohol and residual sugar rates!

However, if for some reason, you absolutely have to know the alcoholic strength of your wine, we propose an easy, effective, and inexpensive method, which consists of taking a density reading of the wine and carrying out a simple experiment.

Carefully measure a small amount of wine (for example, 125 ml. or $^1/_2$ cup), enough to take an S.G. reading with the hydrometer. Write down the result (which we will call I.D. for "initial density"). Simmer the wine in a stainless steel or pyrex cooking vessel until its volume is reduced by half: all the alcohol in it will have evaporated at this point. Add exactly the amount of water necessary to re-establish the precise original liquid volume, then cool the wine to a temperature of 15°C (59°F). Measure the density again (we will call it F.D., for "final density") and write down the result.

Subtract the initial density reading (I.D.) from the final density reading (F.D.). Because the liquid has lost all of its alcohol, the final density is necessarily higher than the initial density; as we have seen, the density of grape must gradually decreases during fermentation as the alcohol rate rises (the density of alcohol being lower than that of water, in a proportion of 0.792 to 1.000). Therefore, the result of the subtraction will always be a positive number. For example, if the F.D. is 1.010 and the I.D. is 0.994, the result of the subtraction is 0.016, or 16. This result corresponds to a given alcohol rate established in the conversion table given below. In the case of our example, the rate is 12.3%.

Alcohol Rate Equivalents

F.D. - I.D.	% Alcohol	F.D. - I.D.	% Alcohol
1.5	1.0	14	10.5
2	1.3	15	11.4
3	2.0	16	12.3
4	2.7	17	13.2
5	3.4	18	14.1
6	4.1	19	15.1
7	4.9	20	16.0
8	5.6	21	17.0
9	6.4	22	18.0
10	7.2	23	19.0
11	8.0	24	20.0
12	8.8	25	21.0
13	9.7	26	22.0

The Brix (or Balling) Density Scale

In the wine industry, whether in France or in the United States, oenologists use the Brix (or Balling) density scale, rather than the specific gravity (S.G.) scale. In both cases, the scale is based on the weight resistance to a certain liquid, but the calibration is different. Most hydrometers include the Brix (or Balling) scale as well as the S.G. scale.

To make it easier for you, we have included a conversion table (on the following page) giving the equivalence between specific gravity readings and Brix (or Balling) readings. The table also includes the sugar weight (in grams per litre) and the potential alcohol rate for each of the readings.

Once you have a density reading, you can use this table to know how much sugar (or dextrose) to add to your must if you want to increase the percentage of alcohol.

The table also includes the equivalence between the Canadian alcohol measurement system (by volume) and the American "proof" system (one Canadian unit corresponds to half a "proof").

Various Tests

Determining the Acidity Rate

It is important to know, first of all, that it is not at all practical to try to measure the acidity rate of the must when it is in ferment, as the presence of carbon dioxide (an acidic gas) can distort the measurement. If it is really necessary to know the acidity rate at this stage, there are two ways to prepare samples for analysis. One is to remove the carbon dioxide by means of a partial vacuum pump (a method which is certainly not accessible to everyone), and the other is to simmer a sample for 5 or 10 minutes to release the carbon dioxide (CO_2). Once the carbon dioxide is removed, it will be

Density, Sugar and Potential Alcohol

Density (S.G.)	Brix	Sugar Oz./U.S. gal.	Sugar g./l.	Potential Proof (%)	Potential Alcohol (%)	Alcohol/vol. (Canada) %	U.S. Degrees Proof
1.000	0.0						
1.005	1.3	0.5	15	1.7	0.8	5	10
1.010	2.6	1.0	27	3.0	1.5	10	20
1.015	3.9	1.4	39	4.3	2.2	15	30
1.020	5.2	1.8	51	5.7	2.8	20	40
1.025	6.5	2.2	63	7.0	3.5	25	50
1.030	7.8	2.6	75	8.3	4.2	30	60
1.035	9.1	3.1	87	9.7	4.8	35	70
1.040	10.4	3.5	99	11.0	5.5	40	80
1.045	11.7	3.9	111	12.3	6.2	45	90
1.050	13.0	4.3	123	13.7	6.8	50	100
1.055	14.3	4.8	135	15.0	7.5	55	110
1.060	15.6	5.2	147	16.3	8.2	60	120
1.065	16.9	5.6	159	17.7	8.8	65	130
1.070	18.2	6.0	171	19.0	9.5	70	140
1.075	19.5	6.5	183	20.3	10.2	75	150
1.080	20.8	6.9	195	21.7	10.8	80	160
1.085	22.1	7.3	207	23.0	11.5	85	170
1.090	23.4	7.7	219	24.3	12.2	90	180
1.095	24.7	8.1	231	25.7	12.8	95	190
1.100	26.0	8.6	243	27.0	13.5	100	200

In the vinification process, a rate of 18 grams of sugar per litre produces about 1 degree of alcohol. The g./l. sugar rate takes the unfermentable particles contained in the wine into account.

possible to obtain precise measurements in the tests described below.

Sodium Hydroxide Test

There is more than one way to determine the acidity content of wine. Several kinds of expensive apparatus exist, but for the purposes of home winemakers, there is a more appropriate little kit which costs about $10 and is available at winemaking speciality shops.

This kit includes a solution of sodium hydroxide, a pH indicator (phenolphtalein), a test tube, and two syringes. The procedures are different for red and for white wine.

In the case of white wine, extract 15 cc. of must with one syringe and inject it into the test tube; add two or three drops of phenolphtalein.

Draw 10 cc. of sodium hydroxide solution into the other syringe, and add it to the test tube, one cubic centimetre at a time. After each cc. of sodium hydroxide, shake the tube a little, and watch for a definite colour change (the solution will turn red or reddish grey). The number of cubic centimetres required to produce this effect is equivalent to the acidity rate in grams. Thus, if six cc. of sodium hydroxide solution are necessary to turn the sample red, it means that the must or the wine contains 6 grams of acid per litre.

For red wine, the procedure differs in that phenolphtalein is not needed for the colour differentiation. The red wine will turn brown or black when all the acid has been neutralized. If the wine is very dark to begin with, you can lighten it by diluting it in twice as much water (30 cc.). This dilution has no effect whatsoever on the result, and it makes the colour change easier to observe.

Sodium Hydroxide and the pH-meter

If you possess a pH-meter[2], the operation is even simpler. You don't need to use phenolphtalein as a pH indicator, and just have to add the sodium hydroxide solution until the pH-meter reads 7. The amount (in cubic centimetres) of sodium hydroxide that was added corresponds to the acidity rate in grams per litre.

Determining the Residual Sugar Rate

It is easy for the home winemaker to procure a kit for determining the rate of residual sugar in the wine: available at any pharmacy, the Clinitest kit is a very accurate, inexpensive sugar-testing kit for diabetics. It contains little tablets which should be kept dry in their original container. The testing procedure is simple, but be careful not to hold the test tube in your hands, as the liquid will heat up very fast. Using the dropper provided in

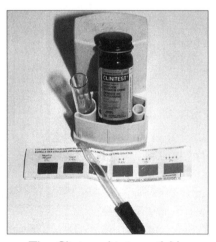

The Clinitest kit is available at the drugstore.

the kit, begin by putting 5 drops of wine into the test tube (also provided). Add 10 drops of water and shake; add one of the tablets, wait 15 seconds, then shake again gently. The solution will turn a colour which clearly matches one of the colours in the grading scale provided in the kit. The precise percentage of sugar is indicated beside each colour. Bright orange indicates 2% of residual sugar; blue-black indicates 0%, etc.

2. See illustration, page 60.

Determining the Sulphur Dioxide Content

A kit named Titrets, made by CHEMetrics and available in winemakers' shops, allows you to evaluate fairly accurately how much sulphur dioxide is in your wine.

Kit to determine the amount of sulphur dioxide in the wine.

You can carry out ten tests with one kit. It contains:

1. hermetically-sealed glass phials containing an iodine-based product;
2. a flexible rubber tube containing phosphoric acid, to be placed over the pointed end of the phial;
3. a titrator, or plastic casing, to hold the phials.

This test may seem complicated when you first try it, but after a few times, it becomes quite routine. The essential point is that air must not enter the phial: therefore the stem of the phial must be inside the wine sample when it is broken open.

The test is carried out in the following way:

- First, slide the rubber tube over the stem of the phial.
- Slide the phial into the titrator. This casing serves not only to hold the phial, but also to break it open and to let in the wine.
- By means of the mechanism built into the titrator, break the stem of the phial (it must be inside the wine). Wine will immediately be drawn into it.
- Work the lever of the titrator a few times to draw small quantities of wine into the phial.
- Continue in this manner, turning the titrator upside-down a couple of times, until the wine's original colour is restored. Red wine, which becomes blackish when it

enters the phial, turns red again, whereas white wine, which becomes grey when it enters the phial, will return to an light amber colour.

- When the colour of the wine in the phial is close to that of the control sample (its original colour), remove the phial from the titrator, hold it stem upwards, and take the reading from the scale on the stem of the phial. The level indicates the parts per million of free sulphur dioxide in the wine.

Altering the Alcohol Rate in Wine

You may want to raise (or lower) the alcohol content in your wine. The best way to do this is by blending wines that have different alcohol contents until the desired rate is achieved. You can also add a little of the pure alcohol sold in liquor stores (unflavoured vodka is also appropriate) and blend it with the wine.

The Pearson Square

The main question is the quantity of alcohol to add to obtain the desired rate. It is easier to calculate this when you can see the formula in diagram form in the Pearson Square.

Let us imagine that a certain wine, which we will call B, has a 10 % alcohol rate, and we would like to increase the rate to 20 % (a rate which we will call C), to make a fortified wine. Let us also suppose that we have a certain quantity of liquor, or spirit (which we will call A) with an alcohol rate of 40 %.

We need to know how much of the spirit we should add to the wine to obtain our desired alcohol rate. The Pearson Square formula is illustrated below.

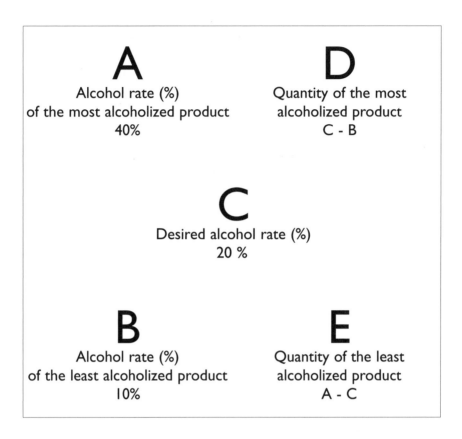

Thus, we have three measurements, three alcohol rates (in %):

A (spirit) = 40
B (wine) = 10
C (desired rate) = 20

To obtain the solution to our problem, we simply have to apply the subtraction formulae that are found to the right of A and B, that is, the ones that are indicated by the letters D and E:

if D = C - B, this makes: 20 - 10 = 10
if E = A - C, this makes: 40 - 20 = 20

The answer that we are looking for is: ten parts of spirit at 40 % alcohol (A), and 20 parts of wine at 10 % alcohol (B) are needed to obtain a wine at 20 % alcohol (C).

To Know the Alcohol Rate of A Blend

You may occasionally want to know the alcohol rate of a blend. For example, if 20 litres of wine at an 12% alcohol rate are blended with 10 litres of wine at an alcohol rate of 8%, what will be the alcohol rate of the resulting mixture? By using the Pearson Square formula, we will arrive at the answer.

A = 12 (20 litres)
Alcohol rate (%)
of the most alcoholized product

D (C - B)
Quantity of the most
alcoholized product

C
Desired alcohol rate (%)

B = 8 (10 litres)
Alcohol rate (%)
of the least alcoholized product

E (A-C)
Quantity of the least
alcoholized product

The formula used here is a bit complicated, especially if you have forgotten your algebra. But if you follow the steps below, you won't have any trouble when you use it to calculate your own blends.

Let us state the Pearson Square formula again, that is: D = C - B.

We know the value of D (20 litres) and of B (8%). Thus we have 20 = C - 8.

If we want to calculate the rate for one litre, the formula will be:

$$\frac{20}{20} = \frac{C-8}{20} \quad \text{Therefore,} \quad 1 = \frac{C-8}{20}$$

Now, as we know that E = A - C, and that the value of E is 10 litres and that of A is 12%, we can write:

$$10 = 12 - C$$

Making the calculation for one litre, we obtain:

$$\frac{10}{10} = \frac{12-C}{10} \quad \text{Therefore,} \quad 1 = \frac{12-C}{10}$$

To find the value of C (the alcohol rate of the blend, in %), we can simply resolve the equation this way:

$$\frac{C-8}{20} = \frac{12-C}{10}$$

$$\frac{20 \times (C-8)}{20} = \frac{(12-C) \times 20}{10}$$

$$C - 8 = (12 - C) \times 2$$
$$C - 8 = 24 - 2C$$

$$C - 8 + 8 = 24 - 2C + 8$$
$$C = 32 - 2C$$

$$C + 2C = 32 - 2C + 2C$$
$$3C = 32$$

$$C = \frac{32}{3}$$
$$C = 10.7\%$$

CHAPTER 8

Grape Varieties and Home-Made Wine

n this chapter, we will describe the grape varieties that are most often chosen to make wine (for both industrial and home production). As we explained in Chapter 5 and elsewhere in this book, in most countries, there is no clear legislation controlling the use of the names of grape varieties in the domain of home winemaking. Although the companies that sell must are not allowed to directly label their product "Bordeaux" or "Burgundy", they may still call them "Bordeaux type" or "Burgundy type".

As we know, these labels do not mean that the must even comes from the Bordeaux or the Burgundy regions; it simply indicates that the wine produced from the must will taste somewhat like Bordeaux or Burgundy wine. These musts or concentrates are, for the most part, consitituted of grape varieties that have little in common with Cabernet Sauvignon grapes, which are grown in the greater part of the vineyards of the Bordeaux region, or Pinot Noir grapes, which are the basis of many Burgundy wines. The must labelled a "Bordeaux type" will most likely be composed of a more humble variety, such as the Carignan grape, one of the leaders in world production, or, if it is for white wine, it may be made up of the Ugni Blanc variety, another very widely-grown wine grape (fourth in the world in terms of quantity grown).

The people in the business of selling must buy their grapes wholesale in the world marketplace. Their objective is to achieve the best possible quality at the lowest possible price. It is now easier for them to reach this goal: there has been a phenomenal increase in world grape production over the last twenty-five years, resulting in an overproduction of wine grapes in general, and even an overproduction of the great classic grape varieties. Several countries that used to have a strictly domestic market for their wine grapes have now become serious international competitors in the export market: Australia, Chile, Argentina, the U.S.A. (California), and Russia, to name a few.

We have included fifty of the grape varieties most commonly used, or best-known for winemaking. This is not intended to be an exhaustive list—far from it. But all the great classic varieties appear here, as well as the semi-classic varieties, and the 20 bulk varieties that are most often sold for winemaking purposes. Some will be familar to you; others, less so. Did you know that the Airén grape is the most widely-grown wine grape in the world? Or that Thompson Seedless (which are the grapes used for raisins, including Sultana) are often used as one of the blending components in concentrated musts? Although Thompson Seedless grapes produce an undistinguished wine, they attenuate the harshness of concentrates made from grape varieties with an overbearing flavour.

The grape varieties presented here produce variable results, depending on the regions where they are grown. The grapevine can adapt to any temperate climate, but the way its fruit grows and ripens is strongly influenced by the amount of sun it recieves and the particular properties of the soil. The influence of these factors is quite astonishing, sometimes making it impossible to recognize that grapes grown in different regions are actually of the same variety. This is the case, as we will also mention below, of the Melon de Bourgogne grape, which is used in making Muscadet wine: when it was moved to California, it underwent a spectacular transformation (for the better!). Also, some rather humble varieties have produced exceptional wines when their cultivation and vinification have been carried out with great care and expertise (including the delay of the grape harvest, in some cases).

For these reasons, each must put on the market by a producer is never exactly the same as a must of the same generic name made by a competitor. This is true even when the grapes of the two musts in question come from the same region, and are harvested at the same time. The difference may be due to the attentiveness with which a particular producer has selected the grapes, to the care with which they were transported (or processed on the spot) in optimal storage conditions, and to harmonious blending with other complementary varieties. Another producer may have carried out the same procedures with less care, resulting in a lower-quality must.

Therefore, if you wish to make the best possible choices for your own home-made wine, you will have to seek those retailers who can best inform you of the different musts available. However, be warned: as in every other commercial domain, there is a certain amount of cut-throat competition in the marketing of products for home winemaking. Some wholesalers manage to persuade retailers to sell their products exclusively (by various means, fair or foul). This, of course, does not affect the retailer's ability (and responsibility) to give you all the pertinent information about the products sold in the store, including the processing methods used, and the best ways to get good value from them. Don't hesitate to ask any questions that you may have.

Fifty Wine Grape Varieties

• AIRÉN (red and white, ordinary): few people know that Airén is the world's most widely-grown wine grape. Spread over more than a million acres in La Mancha, in south-central Spain, Airén is used for red as well as white wines. Until about twenty years ago, this variety produced a wine of doubtful quality that contained too much alcohol. However, since the beginning of the 1980s, it has been treated with greater care and fermented using modern methods. The results have been pleasantly surprising: the wine now produced is clean and fruity, with a medium body. It is harvested as early as the end of August to obtain a lower sugar content; this has decreased the wine's previous very high alcohol rate to 13% or 14%.

Airén is used to lighten red wines that are too thick and heavy.

• ALICANTE BOUSCHET (red, ordinary): this grape variety was developed in the 19th century by Bouschet (and son) to serve as a tinting grape (to pigment red wines). It has been spectacularly successful in this respect. Because of that success, and because of its high yield, it has overtaken most of its competitors. It ranks 11th in world production; it is grown in Europe, North Africa, and California.

It is not a great variety. On the contrary, wine made exclusively from Alicante Bouschet grapes is insipid, flabby, and has an unstable colour.

• ALIGOTÉ (white, semi-classic): this variety is the poor cousin of the Chardonnay grape, although some wine-lovers swear by Bourgogne Aligoté wine. The main reproach made against it concerns its lack of body and excessive acidity. Apart from France, Aligoté grapes are grown in Eastern Europe and in California, where they are used to make commercial brands of "coolers."

• BARBERA (red, ordinary): this grape is native to Piedmont (northwestern Italy) and was introduced to the United States at the end of the 19th century. It makes a heavy wine, rather tannic, and dark-coloured. There is some speculation in California that if this grape were grown in a cooler region than the San Joaquin Valley, excellent wines might be the result. This opinion is based on the fact that it has produced some high-quality wines when grown in optimal conditions.

At present, it is mainly used for blending, to give more oomph to insipid wines.

• BOBAL (red, ordinary): this grape variety is grown in large quantitites in Spain. It produces a wine of a very deep red. It is used mostly for blending, contributing to the composition of concentrated and semi-concentrated musts.

• CABERNET FRANC (red, semi-classic): this is the somewhat despised cousin of the Cabernet Sauvignon grape. Although it is not very rich in tannin and acidity, it still produces a very aromatic wine, with a bouquet of raspberry and violet, very pleasant to drink. Its interesting qualities unfortunately disappear when it is blended with other wines, particularly with Cabernet Sauvignon.

This is nevertheless its main function in the California wine industry, where Cabernet Sauvignon is infinitely more favoured. This is a pity, as Cabernet Franc has more potential than is generally recognized.

• CABERNET SAUVIGNON (red, classic): a noble variety of wine grape, Cabernet Sauvignon serves as the basis for most of the great Bordeaux reds. Cabernet Sauvignon demonstrates a balance that cannot be found in any other wine. Its flavour, structure, complexity, and potential for longevity all mark it as a wine for aging: the fine wines made from this variety are obligatorily aged from five to ten years before drinking. It has a wonderfully complex nose of cherry, blackcurrent, and raspberry, with hints of green pepper and occasionally, tobacco.

This variety is becoming increasingly common in the United States. It is grown as much on the East Coast (particularly on Long Island) as it is in California, where excellent wines are made from it in the most temperate regions of the state. In the warmer regions of California, its alcohol content is a bit too high, and its acidity is a little too evident. Cabernet Sauvignon grapes are also widely grown in Australia, Argentina, Chile, Italy, and New Zealand.

• CARIGNAN (red, semi-classic): there is no doubt that this is the variety that produces the most red wine in the world (although it only ranks 5th in the quantity grown) and the one which makes up the largest proportion of grapes in concentrated and semi-concentrated musts. The Carignan variety produces a strongly-coloured wine, rich in tannin and alcohol. It is used for blending, to give more body to wines which are deficient in it.

• CHARDONNAY (white, classic): also known by the name of Pinot Chardonnay, this wine grape variety is grown in huge quantities in the Champagne region, where it is used to make the wine called Blanc de Blancs. It is also found in the Chablis subregion and other parts of Burgundy. It is the basic variety in Mâcon, Meursault, Montrachet and Pouilly-Fuissé wines.

Over the past 20 years, Chardonnay has become the cosseted darling of wine-growers. Endowed with a good amount of acidity, it has apple, lemon, melon, and pineapple fruits, and notes of butter, hazel-nut, and vanilla. It ages well in a cellar for several years.

The demand for Chardonnay grapes is so high that its price has become almost prohibitive. Easy to cultivate, it has spread all over the world; particularly large quantities are grown in Australia and South Africa.

In the United States, it produces wines with a lot of character and fruity, lemony scents. Chardonnay is a wine that definitely gains by maturing in oak casks. It is also one of the rare white wines that should undergo malolactic fermentation.

• CHASSELAS (white, grown in small quantities): this variety is found in Switzerland, France, and New Zealand. It is mainly used to produce a Swiss wine, also known as Perlan.

• CHENIN BLANC (white, semi-classic): this wine grape variety, very common in France, is also called Pinot de la Loire. Chenin Blanc is a nervous and lively wine, with intense floral, lemon, and even melon scents. This grape variety is capable of producing remarkable and varied vintages, from dessert wines to dry wines. It also make excellent sparkling wines!

When it leaves its native shores, Chenin Blanc does not travel very well: many of its best qualities are lost, and it becomes a humble, although good, table variety. None the less, it is grown almost all over the world, in South Africa (where it is used to make sherry, port, and brandy), in New Zealand, in Australia (where it is mistakenly called Sémillon), in Argentina and Chile, and in the United States.

• CINSAUT, also written CINSAULT (red, semi-classic): a grape variety from the south of France. It is mainly used as a blending component in Côtes du Rhône wines. It is popular in Lebanon and South Africa, where it is used to make table wine.

• CLAIRETTE RONDE: see UGNI BLANC.

• COLOMBARD (white, ordinary): although this variety has been losing ground in its native Charentais, north of Bordeaux, French Colombard is very popular in the United States for the pleasant dry, semi-sweet, and blended wines that are made from it. It is widely used for "coolers" and "champagnettes," and is occasionally blended with Chenin Blanc. It makes quite a good wine, lively, with good acidity, a bit spicy, with floral notes.

• CÔT (red, ordinary): this red-wine grape variety, also called Malbec, is mainly used in blending with Bordeaux wines to produce claret. Rich in tannins, aroma, and colour, it is an admirable complement to lighter varietals. It is the jewel in the crown of Cahors, where it has become the emblem wine of that region. It is also grown in Chile, Argentina, and Australia.

• FOLLE BLANCHE (white, grown in small quantities): a grape variety used mainly in the elaboration of cognac, as well as for Muscadet wines in the western part of the Loire valley.

• FRENCH COLOMBARD: see COLOMBARD.

• GAMAY (red, semi-classic): the grape variety of predilection in the Beaujolais region. It produces a wine of a purple-red colour, with quite a high acidity rate, but little tannin. Its main characteristic is its bouquet in which a plethora of fruits burst forth. It is not as fine as the Pinot Noir grape of the same region, but it is still an excellent variety, with the added benefit of longevity.

Not to be confused with NAPA GAMAY (see below).

- GARNACHA (see GRENACHE, below).
- GEWÜRZTRAMINER (white, classic): this celebrated Alsace variety is a hybrid of Traminer grapes. It creates a powerful, well-structured wine with an intense nose. Its name is evocative (*Gewürz* means spice), it releases scents of lychee and lavender, enhanced by undertones of clove and nutmeg.

It is also grown in northern Italy (it is believed that the Traminer grape originated there), Austria, and Germany, as well as in Eastern Europe (Slovenia, the Czech Republic, Hungary, and Romania), New Zealand and Australia.

Gewürztraminer wines produced in the United States have not been impressive so far, especially in the warmer regions, where the grape's acidity rate becomes too low.

- GRENACHE (red, ordinary): Grenache takes second place in world grape cultivation and first place in its native Spain (where it is called Garnacha). It is very often used for blending. The wine is a light red which nevertheless possesses a solid structure and a high alcohol content (15% or 16%). The variety is also widely grown in the south of France and in California. It is used in the production of several Côtes du Rhône wines, and is blended with Mourvèdre and Cinsaut to produce the famous Châteauneuf du Pape.
- JOHANNISBERG RIESLING: see RIESLING.
- JURANÇON (red, grown in small quantities): this grape variety is grown in the Cahors region, east of Bordeaux, to make wines for local consumption. When blended with Malbec and Merlot, it produces robust wines with a pronounced aroma. Without blending, however, this varietal is bitter and inky.
- LEMBERGER, or LIMBERGER (red, grown in small quantities): an Austrian wine grape variety known in its homeland as Blaufränkisch (or Blauer Lemberger/Limberger), it is also grown in Washington State. It produces wines ranging from a pale pink to a clear ruby. It has a high acidity and an exhuberant, spicy aroma.
- MALBEC (red, ordinary): see CÔT, above.

- MALVASIA (white, ordinary): one of the oldest known wine-grape varieties, originating in Asia Minor. Its present name evolved from "Monemvasia," the name of a port in the Peloponnesus. It is an excellent variety grown throughout the world, although it is rapidly losing ground to Ugni Blanc, which produces table wines that can be drunk younger than those made from Malvasia grapes. This is not a particularly positive development, as Malvasia, also used for making port, ages very well and is much more distinguished than the Ugni Blanc bulk variety.
- MALVOISIE (white, ordinary): with Muscat and Malvasia, Malvoisie is among the oldest wine-grape varieties cultivated today. It produces a very good wine, although unfortunately, it is losing favour in these times, with so many people choosing to drink younger, lighter wines. It is still widely grown in Europe, perhaps because these older, longer-maturing varieties are better appreciated there.
- MATARO: see MOURVÈDRE, below.
- MELON DE BOURGOGNE (white, semi-classic): better known as Muscadet, Melon de Bourgogne is hardly found anymore in the Burgundy region of its origins. However, it has adapted very well in the Loire valley, where the famous Muscadet Sèvres-et-Maine is matured *sur lie* (allowed to mature on its lees, or yeast sediment). It produces a very dry wine with a light, floral bouquet. It must be drunk young, as it does not age well.

This variety is grown in California under the name of Pinot Blanc. Transplanted into another climatic zone and grown with ultra-modern techniques, California Pinot Blanc is now astonishingly different from its parent variety. This new breed of Melon de Bourgogne produces surprisingly good, rich wines which age quite well for several years.

- MERLOT (red, classic): considered inferior to Cabernet Sauvignon grapes, Merlot is still a great red-wine grape variety. We shouldn't forget that it alone accounts for 95% of the composition of Château Petrus! Fruity, ample, and nicely tannic, with a bouquet of blackcurrant, cherry, and mint, Merlot is quite self-sufficient, although it blends harmoniously with Cabernet Sauvignon.

Merlot grapes do not travel as well as their Cabernet Sauvignon counterparts, but they can be found in a wide variety of wine-producing regions in Eastern Europe, California, Chile, Argentina, and New Zealand. This grape variety is extensively grown in Italy, where it makes very good wines.

In California, oddly enough, Merlot is sometimes confused with the Cabernet Franc variety.

• MISSION (red, ordinary): this grape variety is one of the first to be imported to the New World. It was planted by Spanish Jesuits (although some people claim that they were Franciscans!) in California in the 17th century. It produces a very fleshy wine with a high alcohol content. It is believed to be a descendant of the Monica grape which is grown in Spain and Sardinia. Although the wine made from it is rather ordinary, it is grown abundantly in all the main wine-producing regions of the world, especially in North America. Mission grapes grown in Chile are known by the name of Pais. This variety occupies sixth place in world production, and is used mainly for blending.

• MONASTRELL (red, ordinary): the second most widely-grown wine grape in Spain, after the Grenache variety, and 9th in the world. The advantage of Monastrell is that it is easy to grow: it tolerates hot weather well, and is even resistant to phylloxera! The fruit is small and sweet, producing highly alcoholic wines that are rather flabby and pale.

• MONTEPULCIANO (red, ordinary): originally a Tuscan grape, Montepulciano is now grown in many other parts of Italy, especially in the centre and the south. Not very acidic but sufficiently tannic, with a robe of a rich, deep red and a blackberry scent with notes of pepper and spices, Montepulciano wines are supple, mellow wines which age beautifully.

This variety is often blended with Sangiovese to produce a fruity wine with a pleasant aroma, rounded and perfectly balanced. An excellent variety for winemaking.

• MOURVÈDRE (red, ordinary): this variety is grown mostly in the southern part of the Rhône valley. It is used in blending to give more body and colour to feebler wines. It is not grown very much in California, where it is sometimes called Mataro. In North America, Mourvèdre is said to have a green tea herbaceous flavour; its nose is qualified as "animal" by the French.

• MOSCATO: see MUSCAT, below.

• MÜLLER-THURGAU (white, ordinary): a cross between Riesling and Sylvaner, the Müller-Thurgau is the most abundantly-grown wine grape in Germany, and has spread throughout the wine-producing world. It is the basic wine grape for the majority of wines produced in New Zealand, and occupies a place of honour in Hungary and Austria. Alone, it produces a respectable wine which, however, has been criticized for its animal nose (some people say that it gives off an odour of cat, or even mouse!). A small quantity of Müller-Thurgau is grown in North America.

• MUSCADET: see MELON DE BOURGOGNE, above.

• MUSCAT (white and red, semi-classic): called Muscat de Frontignan in France and Moscato di Canelli in Italy, this variety ranks 8th in world production. Its very distinctive taste and bouquet cannot be mistaken. Its best-known wines are sweet and semi-sweet vintages, but it can also make good red and white table wines. There is a wide range of Muscat wine grapes: Muscat of Alexandria, Muscat Ottonel, and Muscat Hamburg, among others.

• NAPA GAMAY (red, ordinary): Napa Gamay (or Gamay 15) grapes are grown extensively in the Napa and Monterey regions, and produce some superlative California wines. However, the name is misleading: oenologists have classified Napa Gamay as a clone [1] of Pinot Noir and not a true

---

1. Cloning is the modern way of propagating grape varieties. It consists in selecting the best vine branch of a variety and planting a whole vineyard with graftings from it. The resulting plants will be genetically identical to the parent vine, and will have the same resistant properties.

Gamay variety. It is also called Gamay Noir and Gamay Beaujolais. It produces a heavy, rich, and strongly-coloured wine. Depending on the individual producer, it is sold either as Gamay or as Pinot Noir.

• NEBBIOLO (red, semi-classic): grown mostly in Italy, this great wine-grape variety produces red wines which are considered among the best in the world; it is sometimes classified as a noble variety. In spite of this, Nebbiolo is not grown in many parts of the world, which is our loss.

• PETITE SIRAH (red, ordinary): some wine experts have claimed that Petite Sirah, as it is grown in California, is completely unrelated to the Syrah grown in the valley of the Rhône and in Australia. It has also been said that this variety is actually a hybrid called Durif. Today, the experts are much less categorical on this subject.

Whatever the case may be, Petite Sirah produces a tannic wine of a deep hue, robust and fleshy, very peppery and perfumed, with good aging potential. An interesting wine grape with unexploited possibilities, it is also blended with Zinfandel to give the resulting wine greater complexity.

• PINEAU DE LA LOIRE: see CHENIN BLANC.

• PINOTAGE (white, semi-classic): one of the most celebrated South African varieties, a hybrid of Pinot Noir and Cinsaut. It produces wine of an intense aroma and "roasted" flavour. It has good colour and ages well.

• PINOT BLANC (white, semi-classic): notwithstanding the different arguments concerning its origins, it seems that the Pinot Blanc grape is a close relative of Pinot Noir, just as the Pinot Gris grape is.

Pinot Blanc is often used as a table wine, or for blending. It is full-bodied, but is rather lacking in aroma, unless we count a light spiciness with a hint of Muscat scent. It is grown in Alsace, Germany, Italy, and Eastern Europe.

In Chile and Australia, wine is made from a grape known as Pinot Blanc, but it is doubtful whether it is the true Pinot Blanc variety.

In the United States, an excellent wine labelled Pinot Blanc is actually made from Melon de Bourgogne grapes.

- PINOT CHARDONNAY: see CHARDONNAY.

- PINOT GRIS (red, semi-classic): Pinot Gris grapes have been known since the Middle Ages, when they were cultivated in Burgundy. Like Pinot Blanc, Pinot Gris wines are full-bodied, but have little aroma. This does not prevent the Italians from cherishing their Pinot Grigio wines, and the Hungarians from venerating their Pinot Gris wines, which are made to resemble Tokay by leaving the grapes on the vine as long as possible before harvesting them.

Elsewhere in the world, from North America to Australia, this grape is under-represented in wine production.

- PINOT NOIR (red, classical): the greatest red-wine grape of Burgundy, it generally produces rich, fruity wine with marked cherry, strawberry and raspberry flavours. It ages well and can be preserved for many years, after which it develops a delicious bouquet of chocolate, venison, figs, and truffles. Pinot Noir is also used in the preparation of Champagne.

Some people prefer it to Cabernet Sauvignon, which they find too austere in comparison. Grown in small acreages throughout the world, its regions of predilection are in Australia and the United States (California and Oregon).

- RIESLING (white, classic): grown mainly in Germany and Austria, this grape variety produces one of the world's best white wines, although its cultivation is prohibited in France. Fruity, slender and elegant, Riesling wines have a floral aroma with scents of apple, apricot, and even peach! It has a desirable acidity and ages wonderfully.

In other wine-producing regions of the world, Riesling is often confused with other varieties (Sémillon, for one). California Riesling grapes produce spicy, fruity wines.

- RKATSITELI (white, ordinary): surprisingly for those who are not familiar with Eastern varieties, Rkatsiteli, which originates in Turkey and Armenia, is the third most widely-grown wine grape in the world. It is now grown largely in

Eastern Europe, especially in Russia, and produces quite good table wines resembling Rieslings and Gewürztraminers.

In the Western Hemisphere, it is found mainly in the Finger Lakes region of New York State.

• RUBY CABERNET (red, ordinary): a hybrid of Carignan and Cabernet Sauvignon, Ruby Cabernet is grown mostly in California, where it has adapted very well. Ruby Cabernet grapes are used as tinting grapes, and for blending in the production of light, unpretentious table wines. Alone, it becomes a tannic, fruity wine with a dark robe. It is also grown in Argentina, Chile, Australia, and South Africa.

• SAINT-ÉMILION: see UGNI BLANC, below.

• SANGIOVESE (red, semi-classic): this variety grows in Tuscany and is the basis for Chianti wines. In the best of conditions, wine made from Sangiovese grapes can resemble a very good Bordeaux vintage. It is not a wide-spread variety, although it is now in the process of being implanted in California; it has produced some well-balanced wine there, and hopes are high for its development.

• SAUVIGNON BLANC (white, classic): this variety produces some excellent Sancerre and Pouilly-Fumé wines. Even though Sauvignon Blanc is not reputed to age well (it should be drunk within two years of bottling), it is still increasingly appreciated because its characteristics correspond to the image of 20th-century modernity: it is a dry and nervous wine, thirst-quenching and refreshing. It has a very aromatic nose with herbaceous notes.

• SÉMILLON (white, classic): grown all over the world, Sémillon is often used for blending purposes. However, by itself, it produces excellent wine: for example, Hunter Valley, an Australian Sémillon.

Sémillon is not grown very much in the Unted States, as Chardonnay and Riesling grapes are preferred for white wines; American Sémillon wines are of a respectable quality, but are rather limp.

• SHIRAZ: see SYRAH, below, or PETITE SIRAH, above.

- SYRAH (red, classic; see also PETITE SIRAH, above): this wine grape is grown almost exclusively in the Rhône valley, where excellent Hermitage and Côte Rôtie wines are made from it. Very popular among wine-growers in Australia, accounting for 40 % of the red wine grapes grown there, Syrah produces a wine of a very dark colour, often referred to as inky. Robust, fleshy and tannic, Syrah is a wine with a generally unappreciated potential.

- SYLVANER (white, ordinary): this variety is losing ground these days because of its absence of nose. It produces a rather insipid wine, which is none the less very pleasant to drink because of its lightness. In fact, it is lacking in neither body nor acidity. As it does not have much of a bouquet, it may soon be left behind by varieties with more character.

- THALIA: see UGNI BLANC.

- THOMPSON SEEDLESS (white, ordinary): among the most widely-grown wine grape varieties in California, where a phenomenal quantity is grown in the San Joaquin Valley. Of course, it is a very popular table grape and raisin grape, as well as a wine grape. The wine does not have much flavour, and is used for attenuating the too-strong taste of certain wines.

- TOCAI FRIULANO (white, grown in small quantities): limited to the Friuli region of northeastern Italy, this Tokay variety produces light wines with a floral and hazel-nut bouquet, for drinking very young. It is believed that this grape is grown in Chile under the name Cabernet Vert.

Transplanted to the United States, it produces a wine with intense perfumes of underripe fruits. It has a medium acidity. Vintners often use it to make fat and mellow dessert wines.

- TRAMINER (white, semi-classic): this name was given to the Gewürztraminer variety until the beginning of this century, and is still occasionally used.

- TREBBIANO: see UGNI BLANC, below.

- UGNI BLANC (white, semi-classic): the Ugni Blanc grape ranks 4th in world production. It goes under several names, depending on where it grows (Saint-Émilion and Clairette in France, Trebbiano in Italy, Thalia in Portugal, and White Shiraz in Australia). It is easily grown, and produces nicely acidic, clean, pleasant-tasting and unpretentious wines, which are also used for blending to contribute acidity, or to attenuate heaviness. It is also used in France in the making of cognac.

• VERDICCHIO (white, ordinary): this variety owes its name to the greenish-yellow colour of its grapes. It has largely remained in its native Italy, where it has been grown since the 15th century in the Ancona and Macerata regions. Even though it has not emigrated very much, it is grown in such large quantitities that it now ranks 15th in world grape cultivation. It is not particularly easy to grow, and produces rather characterless wines, but its high acidity makes it an ideal variety for sparkling wines.

• WELSCHRIESLING (white, ordinary): although "Riesling" is part of its name, this variety does not originate in Germany, where moreover, it is generally the object of derision! It is believed to be a variety of French origin. It generally produces wines that are not very acidic and do not have much body, but which are very aromatic. When the grapes are harvested very late, as is the practice in northeastern Italy and in Austria, the resulting wines are superb.

Welschriesling grapes rank 16th in world production, and are grown mainly in Eastern Europe (Romania, Bulgaria, Hungary, and in regions of the former Yugoslavia). The wine is widely used for blending.

• WHITE SHIRAZ: see UGNI BLANC, above.

• ZINFANDEL (red, ordinary): the origin of the Zinfandel grape is obscure; no one knows from where it was imported to the United States. Although a DNA analysis recently showed that it belongs to the same family as the Primitivo d'Apulia variety of southern Italy, Zinfandel fanatics persist in giving a greater mystique to its pedigree, claiming that it predates the Apulian variety!

This is a versatile wine grape: it is the basis for table wine, for rosés, and for quite exceptional reds. It has infinite possibilities. Vintners have established its credentials by producing wines that are firmly-structured and robust with elderberry flavours, often spicy and peppery. Strongly tannic with good alcoholic strength, deep and complex, this is a wine that could have the same longevity as the Cabernet Sauvignon variety. And that's saying a lot!

Bibliography

ASSINIWI, Bernard, *Faites votre vin vous-même*, Montreal, Bibliothèque québécoise (BQ), 1994, 210 p.

AUBRY, Jean et Véronique DHUIT, *L'abécédaire des vins, bières, cidres et spiritueux*, Montreal, Les Éditions Logiques, 1996, 304 p.

BEZZANT, Norman, *The Big Book of Wine*, Secausus, N.J., Chartwell Books Inc., 1985, 400 p.

DEBUIGNE, Dr Gérard, *Larousse les vins*, Paris, Larousse, 1991, 338 p.

DUSSINE, Pierre, *Comment faire de bons vins*, Paris, Flammarion, 1976, 454 p.

FADIMAN, Clifton et Sam AARON, *Wine Buyers Guide*, New York, Harry N. Abrahams Inc. Publishers, 1977, 168 p.

JOHNSON, Hugh, *Le guide mondial du connaisseur du vin. Vins, vignobles, vignerons*, Paris, Robert Laffont, 1983, 546 p.

JOBÉ, Joseph, ed., *Le grand livre du vin*, Lausanne, Edita, 1982, 534 p.

LICHINE, Alexis, *Vins et vignobles de France*, Paris, Robert Laffont, 1979, 514 p.

PEYNAUD, Émile, *Le goût du vin. Le grand livre de la dégustation*, Paris, Dunod, 1980, 242 p.

PEYNAUD, Émile, *Connaissance et travail du vin*, new revised edition, Paris, Dunod, 1984, 342 p.

PEYNAUD, Émile *et al.*, *Traité d'œnologie. Sciences et techniques de vin*: vol. 1, *Analyse et contrôle des vins*, 2nd ed., completely revised and updated, Paris, Bordas/Dunod, 1982, 652 p.; vol. 2, *Caractères des vins. Maturation du raisin.*

Levures et bactéries, 2nd ed., Paris, Bordas/Dunod, 1975, 556 p.; vol. 3, *Vinification. Transformation du vin*, 2nd ed., Paris, Bordas/Dunod, 1976, 722 p.; vol. 4, *Clarification et stabilisation. Matériels et installations*, 2nd ed., Paris, Bordas/Dunod, 1977, 648 p.

RENOUIL, Yves, *Dictionnaire du vin*, Bordeaux, Féret et Fils, 1962, 1346 p.

ROBINSON, Jancis, *Le livre des cépages*, Paris, Hachette, 1988, 282 p.

ROBINSON, Jancis, *Guide to Wine Grapes*, Oxford New York, Oxford University Press, 1996, 240 p.

ROBINSON, Jancis, ed., *The Oxford Companion to Wine*, Oxford/New York, Oxford University Press, 1994, 1090 p.

WOSHEK, H. G., *Les vins*, Paris, Vander Oyez, 1978, 254 p.

Index

Pierre Drapeau was born in Sherbrooke, Quebec, on July 22, 1945. After completing his B.A., he studied chemistry at the Université de Sherbrooke; his long-time love of this science has been extremely helpful ever since he first began making wine in the early 1960s. Now a recognized expert in the field, Mr. Drapeau is very much appreciated by fellow winemakers both as a consultant and as a teacher. Besides continuing his own winemaking activities, he has been the manager of Microvin, a winemaking supply centre, for the past twenty years.

André Vanasse was born in Montreal on March 6, 1942. A critic, novelist and essayist, he has become well-known as the literary director of the successful publishing company, XYZ. André began making wine several years ago and was quickly captivated. Seeing the need for a comprehensive work on home winemaking, he proposed to Mr. Drapeau that they collaborate in writing *The Encyclopedia of Home Winemaking* to provide winemakers with an in-depth reference guide which includes the practical advantages of the most up-to-date methods and all the new equipment available.

Printed in February 2001
by AGMV/Marquis,
Cap-Saint-Ignace (Québec), Canada.